MONTPELIER REGIONAL LIBRARY
RFD #2
MONTPELIER, VT. 05602

WITHDRAWN

Adventure North

The "Fram"

Justin F. Denzel

ADVENTURE NORTH
The Story of Fridtjof Nansen

Illustrated with photographs

Abelard-Schuman   London   New York   Toronto

Copyright 1968 by Justin F. Denzel

Library of Congress Catalogue Card Number: 68-13238

Standard Book Number: 200.71540.2

LONDON	NEW YORK	TORONTO
Abelard-Schuman	Abelard-Schuman	Abelard-Schuman
Limited	Limited	Canada Limited
8 King St. WC2	6 West 57th St.	1680 Midland Ave.

Printed in the United States of America

To Mother and Dad

Acknowledgments

The author and publisher gratefully acknowledge use of the following photographs from the Norwegian Information Service: frontispiece; pages 57; 137; 155; 163; 164; 165; 167.

Thanks also go to John Euller, author of *Arctic World* and *Antarctic World*, published by Abelard-Schuman, for permission to use the two maps which appear in the book.

Contents

1 • Norwegian Boyhood   15
2 • Icebound Seas   29
3 • Plunder of the North   43
4 • Home Is the Sailor   54
5 • The Arctic Calls Again   61
6 • Six Against the North   72
7 • First Across Greenland   84
8 • The Wheel of Ice   99
9 • North with the *Fram*   111
10 • The Long Drift   126
11 • The Trek Toward the Pole   142
12 • The Last Great Adventure   158

Bibliography   169
Index   171

Photographs

Nansen as a youth   17
"Great Fröen" — the dwelling house   21
Seal skinning   37
Male of bladdernose seal   44
Enemy of bladdernose   51
Norwegian fjord   57
Otto Sverdrup   76
Members of Greenland expedition   77
Samuel Balto and Ole Ravna   81
Travelling across inland ice   85
"Sailing" on inland ice   87
Observation taking and dinner on inland ice   91
Godthaab in winter   94
Nansen as young man   103
Colin Archer   112
Designs for the "Fram"   114
The "Fram" leaving Bergen   118
Walrus hunt   120
Sleepy walrus (sketch by Nansen)   121
Reading temperatures with lens   123

Chronometer observation with theodolite   132
Taking deepwater temperatures   133
Taking a sounding   134
"Fram" forcing its way through polar ice   137
Travelling by kayak   148
Heading southward   150
Nansen reaches the kayak   152
Nansen at 36   155
Nansen Passport   163
Visiting refugees in orphanage   164
Nansen in later years   165
"Fram" in Museum at Oslo   167

Adventure North

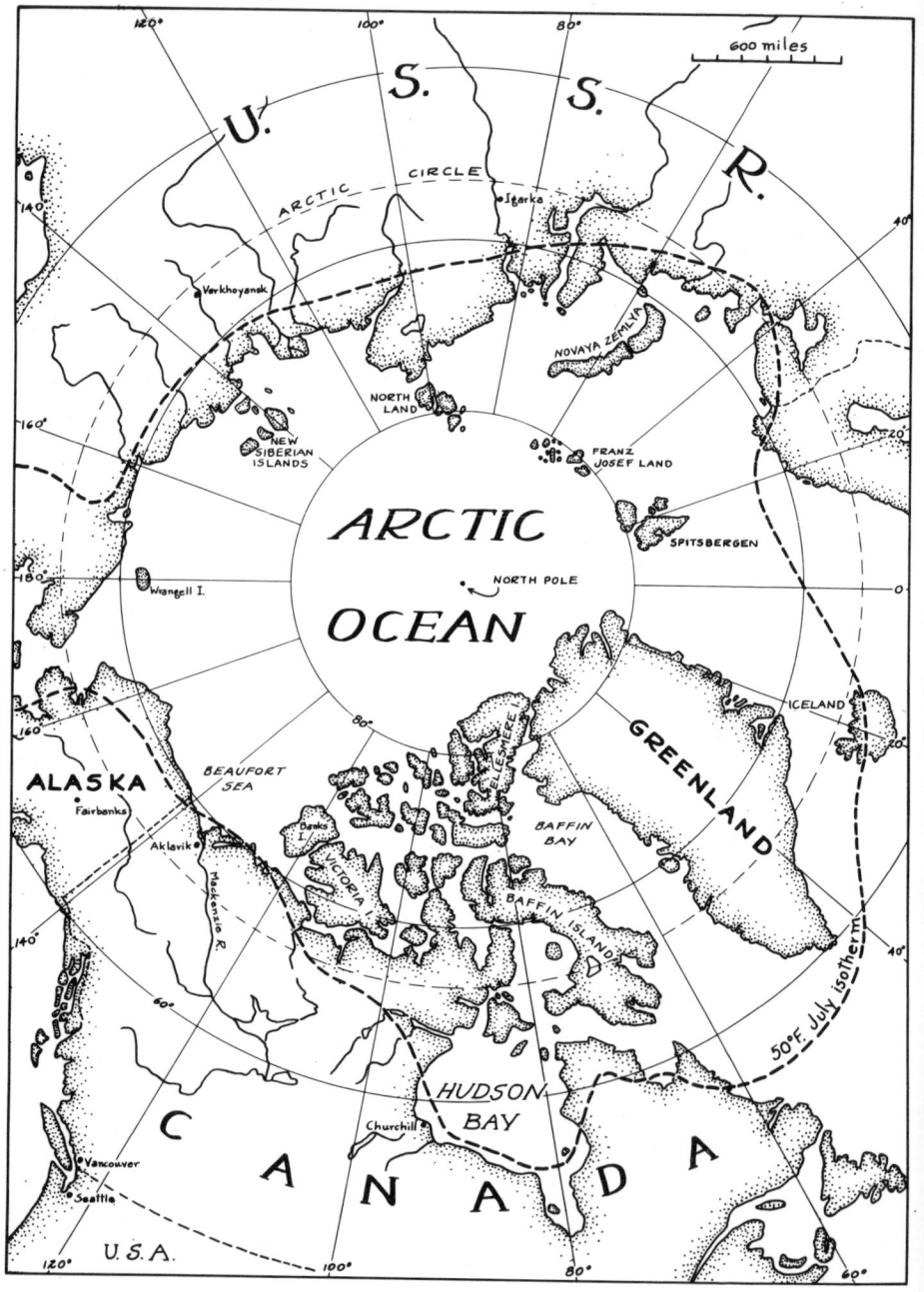

Norwegian Boyhood

A WARM MARCH sun touched the hilltops around Christiania Fjord, bringing them to life in vivid shades of green. In the valley below, the wide inlet of the sea sparkled with animated flashes of white, as herring gulls swooped amid the forests of masts and sails. Here and there patches of snow clung to the edges of the cobblestone streets, the meltwater trickling down the gutters. The very air had a warm, fertile smell as if anticipating an early spring, waiting for the earth to bloom anew.

Fridtjof Nansen walked down Carl John's Street, taking the great strides that suited his six-foot figure. He wore a round beaver hat atop his blond head and a short blue pea jacket with a fur-lined collar. Normally, he would have revelled in this majestic scenery. His poetic soul would have sung deep within himself at this enchanting picture of Norwegian spring.

He had done it a hundred times before on his way to and from classes, but today his active mind was occupied with more immediate adventures.

He proceeded another two blocks, then stopped in front of a large boardinghouse overlooking the fjord. From the inner pocket of his jacket he took out a folded letter and read the address — Captain Alex Krefting, 24 Carl John's Street, Christiania, Norway. He glanced again at the date — February 15, 1882. For three long weeks he had waited for this moment, and now, at last, he would have his answer.

A wave of excitement raced through his veins as he was admitted by a housekeeper and directed to a suite of rooms on the second floor. For the barest fraction of a minute he hesitated, then threw back his shoulders and knocked sharply. He heard the heavy sound of approaching footsteps, and a moment later the door swung open to reveal a huge hulk of a man well over six feet tall with an enormous black moustache and dark piercing eyes.

"Captain Krefting?"

The man stood with his legs wide apart as if bracing himself on the deck of a ship. "Come in, come in," he said, his voice deep and booming.

The young man's eyes glowed with wonder as he entered the big room. There was a thick polar bear rug on the polished floor and another draped over the back of one of the chairs. Hanging on the walls were the mounted heads of walrus and caribou. In the corner, a pair of deer antlers served as a gun rack for an assortment of carbines and rifles. A heavy table stood foursquare in the middle of the room, covered with sailing charts, logbooks and a quadrant.

Slowly the captain took out his pipe and began filling

Nansen as a youth

it from a fat leather pouch, tamping the tobacco down firmly with his thumb. "So you're the young man who wants to go along on a sealing expedition?"

"Yes," said Fridtjof, feeling a bit uneasy under the big man's steady gaze.

"You're a university lad, aren't you?"

"Yes, Sir. I'm a zoology student at Christiania. I thought a trip like this would be a good opportunity to study the animal life of the Arctic — the seals, the whales and that sort of thing."

"Aye, that it would," said Krefting. "But I'm afraid it's not the kind of study you've been used to. It's a dirty business, with long hours and lots of hard work. There are no shiny laboratories up there, you know."

"I realize that," said Fridtjof, hopefully. "I'd go along

as a passenger, of course, but I'd be willing to pitch in and do my share of the work."

Krefting was silent for a moment, staring out of the window at the busy port with its line of grey fishing boats bobbing at their moorings. He tugged thoughtfully at the end of his moustache, mumbling to himself. "It's a bit of a risk."

"You think I'm too young?"

Krefting shrugged. "It's not age that counts. I was only twenty when I had command of my first ship. No; it's something more. A man's got to be hard and tough. When we reach the ice fields we work day and night, getting as many seals as we can, skinning them, loading the pelts on board. It's a cold-blooded occupation measured by results and hard cash, not recommended for the squeamish."

"I'm used to that, Sir. I can handle firearms, and I've done a good bit of hunting."

Krefting looked at this tall, lanky youth with his friendly, open face, his ready smile and willingness to please. He liked what he saw. "How old are you, boy?"

"Twenty-one, Sir."

"Well," he said, finally. "Perhaps there might be time for some hunting and study in between the work. I'm to have a new ship this season, a brand-new ice schooner named the *Viking*." He stopped for a moment, apparently deep in thought.

Fridtjof waited, shifting from one foot to the other.

"Tell you what," Krefting continued. "If you can get permission from the owners, I expect we can make a berth for you."

Fridtjof's heart beat wildly, bursting with anticipation as they discussed the forthcoming voyage in some detail.

When they had finished, he thanked Krefting for his kindness and started for the door.

The big seaman called after him. "We sail out of Arendal on the morning of March eleventh. Better get your gear aboard a day early."

A few days later, Fridtjof's father got in touch with an old friend in Arendal, who talked with the owners of the *Viking*, and in a matter of hours the necessary permission was granted.

Here was the beginning, the first groping attempts of an adventurous youth, a boy who eventually was to become one of the greatest explorers of all time. Possessed of a strong will, relentless determination and keen imagination, his mission was to seek out and explore the last hidden corners of this planet earth.

Two hundred years before him, his great, great, great great-grandfather, one Hans Nansen, had pointed the way with daring voyages into the mysterious White Sea. Without the benefit of maps or instruments, this intrepid man had sailed his little vessel through unknown waters, charting the surrounding coastline for the imperial Czar of Russia. His experiences and exploits led him to write a book on navigation and geography, including the chronology of tides and the declination of the sun and stars, complete with tables, sailing instructions and appropriate excerpts from the Holy Bible. It was a useful book and one that served seafarers long after its author's death. At the age of forty, this same Hans Nansen became burgomaster of Copenhagen and helped organize that city's resistance forces against the ravages of the dreaded tyrant king, Karl Gustav of Sweden.

On his mother's side, Fridtjof could point with pride to the renowned Wedel family, a long line of noblemen, soldiers, statesmen and judges. It was a distinguished clan of rovers and gentlemen, and they left the lad an impressive parade of footsteps in which to follow.

Fridtjof's father, Baldur Nansen, was a small man, slight of build but strong in character and integrity. A competent and gifted lawyer, he earned his living in the handling of property transfer and probate. Mild-mannered, refined and courteous, he was not inclined toward outdoor sports yet did not deny these pastimes to his children.

Fridtjof's mother, on the other hand, was a tall, stately woman of uncommon ability, with a keen zest for living. In spite of an illustrious background, she had no pretensions about birth or nobility and tolerated none in her children. In a day when it was considered unladylike for a woman to indulge in any form of physical activity, she scoffed at convention and enjoyed skiing, hiking and working in the garden.

On October 10, 1861, Fridtjof Nansen was born on the spacious farm estate of Great Fröen, three kilometers from Christiania (now known as Oslo). He grew up in a household full of half brothers and sisters, for both of his parents had been married before. He had one full brother, Alexander, a year younger than himself, who was his constant companion during early childhood.

Here at Great Fröen, with its large, comfortable house, its warm, friendly atmosphere, its courtyards and lawns, there was ample room for a boy to stretch his legs, to wander and to learn. Here were horses and cows, geese and chickens, and huge barns and stables where buggies and sleighs and the sweet scent of fresh hay provided fun and adventure.

In the background were the endless forests of Nord-

"Great Fröen" — the dwelling house

marka, filled with sparkling clear lakes and rippling trout streams. Its willow thickets abounded with ptarmigan and rabbit, its cool, shadowy glades were the home of lynx and deer while its highlands echoed to the mournful cry of the wolf. Along the shores of the lakes and rivers could be found black duck and teal; in the birch stands, goldfinch and siskin twittered in the bright sunlight. To young Fridtjof Nansen it was sheer paradise.

Even at an early age, Fridtjof was an avid reader, and many evenings he and his brother, Alexander, lay on the hearthrug before the light of the fire while their mother read aloud from *Robinson Crusoe,* Asbjörnsen's fairy tales or the exciting stories of Thor and Odin. As he grew older, he discovered the thrilling adventures of the early Arctic explorers, especially the mysterious disappearance of a British admiral, Sir John Franklin, in 1845 and the intrepid voyagers who set out to find him. It was a subject that impressed him immensely and one that was to influence the course of his entire life.

When he was a young boy, he took to hunting squirrels and sparrows with a homemade bow and arrow. His dog Storm chased the quarry up a tree while Fridtjof fired away from below, usually with little success. Even anointing the arrowheads with the juice of poisonous mushrooms failed to produce better results.

In the spring and summer, there were many hours spent fishing for trout in the nearby Frogner River, and on one occasion young Fridtjof came running home fighting tears, a barbed hook embedded in his upper lip. He stood there stoic and taut, with fists clenched tightly at his sides, while his mother cut out the hook with a straight razor.

In the winter there was skating on the frozen ponds, and tobogganing and skiing on the surrounding slopes. Fridtjof patched up a pair of skis that had been lying unused in the attic, and with the first snowfall he started off down the road.

Mr. Fabritius, who lived next door, came riding by in his sleigh. He noticed the youngster's floundering efforts, and pulling his horse over to the side, he tried to stifle a smile.

The boy looked up, grinning. "I'm learning to ski," he shouted. "But I'm not doing too well with these old slats." He held up the skis, broken and out of shape, one longer than the other.

Mr. Fabritius threw back his head and laughed. "No wonder," he said, "even an expert couldn't do much with those." He was silent for a moment, studying the boy's eager face, admiring his courage and perseverance. "Just you wait," he continued. "I'll get you a real pair of skis, then you can learn the right way."

Fridtjof's eyes widened with delight as the man flicked the reins, and horse and sleigh sped off down the road.

The long winter days passed, and Fridtjof waited; but still there were no skis. Spring came and then summer, and finally, with the first sign of autumn frost, Fridtjof could wait no longer. He planted himself in the middle of the road, and as Mr. Fabritius came riding by in his buggy he asked, "I say, what about those skis?"

Without stopping, Mr. Fabritius shouted back over his shoulder, "Don't worry, you'll get them."

Sure enough, one day just before the first fall of snow Fridtjof's sister, Ida, called to him from the front window. "Come quickly," she said, "there's a surprise waiting for you in the house."

Breathlessly he ran inside, and there it was, a long package done up in heavy brown paper.

"Hurry," said Ida. "Open it, I'm dying to see what it is."

With impatient fingers, Fridtjof tore off the wrappings, revealing a pair of glossy red skis. They were made of the finest long-grained ash, beautifully lacquered, with narrow black stripes running down the length. He looked at them proudly, running his hands over the smooth polished curves, holding up the long, shiny ski pole.

Here was the beginning of a new world, a world of space and distance, of speed and excitement. The skis were like magic wings with which he could go soaring over the hills, exploring new valleys, seeking new adventures. Ten kilometers, fifty kilometers would be as nothing.

It was a daily trek of over four miles to and from school, and on the way there were the inevitable scuffles between rival gangs of small boys. Being exceptionally tall and strong for his age, Fridtjof usually stood aloof from such wranglings. But if there was any sign of bullying or unfair play, he waded in with fire in his eyes, doing his utmost to even up the score.

One year a boy came to class who was even bigger than Fridtjof. His name was Karl, and he had an annoying habit of being very domineering and in general making himself obnoxious. Fridtjof took it as long as he could, and then one day during recess, when Karl was hitting the other boys with a soccer ball, he said, "I wouldn't do that if I were you."

Karl drew himself up to his full height. "And just who do you think is going to stop me?"

"I am," said Fridtjof.

There was a tense silence as a crowd of youngsters gathered around, sensing a fight. Suddenly, with a wild throw, Karl flung the ball at Nansen, striking him roughly on the shoulder. That was all Fridtjof needed. He barged in, head down, and the two boys became a blur of flying fists. They battled back and forth across the yard, then fell to the ground, pommelling each other with fists and elbows.

The fight went on a few minutes longer, while the gang of onlookers cheered and shouted encouragement. Suddenly the cheering stopped, and the two boys were lifted bodily into the air. It was Mr. Aars, the burly headmaster, holding each of them firmly by the collar. He hauled them off into the nearest classroom and sat them down behind a desk, facing each other.

"Who started this?" he demanded.

Fridtjof's eyes bore straight ahead. Karl's gaze was on the ceiling.

"All right," said the headmaster. "Since you both refuse to talk you'll just sit there for a while and think it over."

For twenty minutes, Fridtjof stared straight ahead, looking neither to the right nor left. From time to time, Karl shifted uneasily, embarrassed by the long silence. Shyly he stole a glance at Fridtjof, waiting for a sign of recognition. Then suddenly he began to giggle. Fridtjof glared at him, startled. But a moment later he, too, began to see the amusing side of the situation. Together they rocked in their seats, laughing till the tears ran down their faces. And an hour later, when Mr. Aars came back he found them heads together, arms around each other's shoulders, quietly reading a book. From that day on, they became the best of friends.

With time and practice, Fridtjof became an expert skier, though not without the beginner's quota of spills and tumbles. In his first attempt at jumping, he flew through the air, landing headfirst in a snowbank, his legs sticking out in a most comical manner. With an embarrassed grin, he pulled himself out, brushed the snow from his jacket and immediately tried again, this time with better results.

He soon became proficient at downhill runs, jumping and cross-country racing and won many competitions, often against boys older and more experienced than himself.

As Fridtjof grew older, he began to spend more and more time wandering through the forests of Nordmarka, hunting black duck along the rivers and fjords, gunning for woodcocks in the marshes. In the spring, he and Alexander often lived for days at a time in a little sod-roofed hut on the shores of Lake Langli. Here, they fished all day, wading in the cold water, their trouser legs rolled up above their knees. At night, they slept soundly, bedded down on a layer of juniper branches. Next morning, they were up at dawn for a breakfast of black coffee.

But Fridtjof loved best the long solitary treks into the surrounding country, revelling in the serene, quiet beauty of the snow-clad forests. It was an experience that refreshed his spirits and provided opportunity for thought and reappraisal.

On these winter jaunts, cold biting winds often swept down out of the rugged Norwegian hills, howling through the birch trees, and stirring up whirlpools of dry, powdery snow. In the uplands, the tall pine forests were deathly still with only the muffled beat of the owl's wing to break the silence. Fridtjof glided along swiftly on his skis, delighting in the spectacular sweep of scenery as late afternoon twilight painted pastel shades of red and pink on the heavy, snow-laden branches. The shotgun held lightly in the crook of his arm, he watched as his big red setter ranged back and forth across the trail ahead.

When he saw the dog stop, freezing in an awkward pose, he knew that game was not far away. He moved up slowly, his gun held at the ready. He had barely reached the willow thicket when suddenly, with a wild burst of speed, a ptarmigan flew into the air heading for the opposite slope. With careful aim Fridtjof fired, the sharp report echoing through the silent hills. Momentarily, the bird faltered, then tumbled to the ground, its pure white plumage flecked with spots of crimson. In a dozen strides, the big setter pounced on the bird and brought it back to the boy.

Minutes later, a small fire was crackling brightly under the shelter of the tall pines. The ptarmigan was plucked and dressed, and now the boy held it on a stick, turning it slowly over the embers. When the bird was cooked, he tore the flesh apart, sharing it with the dog along with a portion of bacon he had been carrying tucked under his jacket.

With supper finished, he licked his fingers clean, melted a handful of snow in the palm of his hand and drank the water. For a long while, he sat there gazing into the dying embers, deep in thought. Then he scooped out a large hollow in the lee of a snowbank, climbed in and went to sleep, his big dog curled up at his feet.

In this way, he frequently lived outdoors for days at a time with nothing but his gun, a fishing line and a box of matches. It was a wild, carefree existence amid magnificent pine forests, thundering cataracts and lofty fjords, and Fridtjof enjoyed it to the full.

When he was sixteen, his mother died, and the family moved from Great Fröen, leaving behind the happy years of childhood. They settled in Christiania, where Nansen attended the Technical High School and achieved outstanding marks in history, science, mathematics and art.

He was a skillful artist and as a youth of sixteen or seventeen acquired the habit of recording his impressions and observations with sketchbook and pencil. He had also become expert in the use of waterpaints and brush, and throughout his life found them a means of relaxation and enjoyment. Wherever he went, whatever he did, he never failed to fill his portfolio with hundreds of original paintings and drawings depicting the sights and experiences he encountered. Many of his friends, some of them professional artists, declared that he possessed a high degree of skill and that he could have distinguished himself in this field had he so desired.

At the age of nineteen, Fridtjof entered Christiania

University, still uncertain as to his choice of a career. He loved the logic and order of mathematics and physics but could never bring himself to accept the quiet, sedentary existence these sciences required. Whatever his future might be, it would have to include some form of physical activity that would take him outdoors.

On the advice of his professors and after many months of serious thought, he decided on the study of marine biology. His curiosity and interest in living things had always been keen, and the thought of travel in the pursuit of strange and unknown forms of life had a decided ring of adventure.

Nansen threw himself into his studies with purpose and enthusiasm, learning to observe, to dissect, to use the microscope and other tools of his trade. His innate ability and dedication must have been evident, for at the end of his first year his zoology teacher, Professor Robert Collett, suggested an unusual research project — a voyage aboard a sealing vessel into the Arctic seas for study and observation.

Fridtjof was intrigued by the idea. Here was a chance to see, at first hand, that mysterious land of the North with its whales and bears, its seabirds and fish. It would be a kind of biological investigation of the entire sealing industry.

Nansen's mind raced ahead, thinking of the new world that had suddenly been opened up before him. It was to be the first truly scientific expedition of his career. A shoestring venture, to be sure, hardly more than a lark. But it was the prelude to a brilliant life of exploration and adventure that, at a later date, would make his name famous throughout the civilized world.

Icebound Seas

IN MARCH, 1882, loaded down with dip nets, bottles, thermometers, dissecting instruments, sketch pads and books, Fridtjof Nansen climbed aboard the *Viking*. The old sealers and shellbacks watching him come aboard must have shaken their heads in amazement — a university student aboard a sealer; it was unheard of!

But Fridtjof was not to be discouraged. He had made up his mind to study and observe everything that came within his reach. At the university, he had come under the influence of a brilliant, inspiring teacher, Professor Henrick Mohn. Mohn was a scientist, a specialist in meteorology and polar air currents. He had taken a fatherly interest in young Nansen and helped him in his choice of careers.

"Investigate all things," Mohn had told him. "Overlook nothing in your quest for knowledge. Grasp every chance for study and observation, and approach each new problem with an open mind. If you do this, you will never be idle, for your work will be all around you."

Now, the golden opportunity was at hand, and Fridtjof was determined to follow Mohn's advice.

With the first faint light of dawn brightening the eastern sky, the *Viking* sailed out of Arendal, her topsails billowing in the breeze, a thin column of smoke issuing from her funnel. Slowly, she made her way down the Skagerrak, and the next day her bows were pitching in the green sea as she began to buck the mountainous waves of the North Atlantic.

Fridtjof was astounded by the vastness of the open sea, amazed by its changing moods. In spite of initial bouts of seasickness he forced himself to stay alert so that he might not miss even a single minute of this new experience. He toured the vessel from stem to stern, from yardarm to fo'c'sle, filling his diary with innumerable sketches and jottings concerning the *Viking*, her fittings and construction.

She was a sturdy vessel of 620 tons, specially designed for navigating in the Arctic ice pack. Her timbers and crossbeams were of double thickness, her rounded bow heavily reinforced with planks of greenheart and oak extending many feet below the waterline. She was bark-rigged with topsails that could be set from the main deck and additionally powered with a 90-horsepower auxiliary engine.

The young scientist made notes, writing everything down in his diary, not realizing that he would use this information one day in building a ship of his own.

Fascinated by the majestic panoply of wind and waves, Fridtjof stood near the bow for hours on end. At night he watched as schools of dolphin came out of the darkness, leaping and playing in the foaming bow wash, leaving glowing trails of phosphorescence in their wake. By day he marvelled at the swooping dives of the sharp-billed gannets and the graceful, effortless flight of the kittiwake gulls.

On the fourth day out, they ran into a howling northwester. Mountainous green seas broke over the forward rails, sweeping across the main deck, rushing like a millrace down the scuppers. Wave after wave loomed up, huge walls of water momentarily towering over the little ship.

Captain Krefting stood near the helm with Fridtjof down on the half deck enjoying the wild, turbulent scene. Suddenly, over the sound of the wind, he heard Krefting shout, *"Look out!"*

All around him, Fridtjof saw men racing for cover, and then, out of the corner of his eye, he saw the reason for their haste. A huge wave was building up on the starboard bow, threatening to engulf the ship. He barely had time to grab hold of the mizzen shrouds when it broke over the side with a tremendous crash, sweeping him off his feet. He hung on desperately, feeling as though his arms were about to be wrenched from their sockets while the furious rush of water surged over and around him, its gurgling flood ringing in his ears. He held his breath for what seemed like an eternity, until the water subsided and the vessel gradually swung back on an even keel.

When it was over, the seamen came out of their hiding places, wet, sputtering and laughing. They were hardy Norsemen, these seal hunters, used to rough weather and raging seas. It was an encounter they had experienced many times before. But to Fridtjof it was all new, wild and exciting.

Day by day, they headed north, and now Fridtjof began to see the big Arctic fulmars, or mallemucks, as the sailors called them, gliding over the water on motionless wings, banking, turning, swinging down into the trough of the waves, then up again in all their infinite grace and beauty, an endless symphony of motion.

That night, they sighted their first sign of ice. Fridtjof rushed up on deck, peering into the darkness. At first he could see nothing, but then gradually, as his eyes became accustomed to the darkness, he saw an enormous white mass looming larger and larger. His heart beat fast as the ice drifted into view, the inky black waters lapping against its jagged sides. As the minutes passed he began to make out more of the drifting floes, rising and falling on the gentle swells.

The captain had come up behind him now and was standing by the railing quietly smoking his pipe. He nodded toward the distant horizon. "Listen," he said.

Fridtjof turned, straining to catch the sound. It was a deep, rumbling noise like the sound of distant thunder.

"It's the beginning of the spring breakup," said Krefting, "the grinding of the ice floes as they pound against each other in the water. Get a ship caught in that ruckus and she'd be crushed to matchwood quicker than you could hoist a sail."

"Even the *Viking*?"

"Aye, even the *Viking*. She's built to cruise the open floes, but she'd not stand a chance in a roaring ice pack. Many years ago an entire whaling fleet got caught in the ice off the coast of Greenland. Every last ship was lost along with 320 men. The few survivors that were left floated on the ice and were picked up off the point at Cape Farewell."

They were silent for a while, man and boy, enjoying

this impressive drama of the Arctic. Fridtjof thrilled to the thought that he was gazing across hundreds of thousands of miles of unexplored territory.

The hour grew late, and Krefting stifled a yawn. "Better go below now, boy, and get some rest. There'll be plenty to see in the morning."

As he said good night and started to walk away, Krefting called after him. "It'll be getting colder now," he said, indicating Fridtjof's light sweater. "You'd be a sight more comfortable dressed in something warmer."

A few minutes later, as he lay in his bunk staring up at the deck beams, Fridtjof realized that Krefting was right. He had been wearing his lightest clothing, perhaps showing off, hoping to impress the men. It was a foolhardy gesture, and in his own indirect way Krefting had been kind enough to warn him about it. Fridtjof smiled to himself. He was beginning to like this gruff, slow-talking mariner.

When Fridtjof came on deck the following morning, a sparkling world of dazzling beauty met his eyes. As far as he could see, the ice fields stretched for hundreds of miles in every direction. Except for the pale, azure-blue sky everything was dazzling white. The ice crags, the pinnacles, the snow-covered ridges, even the feathery wisps of low-hanging clouds blended in perfectly with the white surroundings.

Beautiful, too, were the graceful ivory gulls with delicate rings of scarlet around their dark, beady eyes. In the narrow, open lanes of water, he saw small flocks of guillemots and auks feeding on plankton and other marine life. The birds poked about for a while, splashing and fluttering in the icy waters. Then suddenly, as if by prearranged signal, they rose in a body and flew off in a straight line back to their cliffside homes on the rocky shores of the Jan Mayen Islands a hundred miles away.

For the next three weeks the *Viking* spent her time searching for the breeding grounds of the seals. Sometimes alone, sometimes with other vessels, she sailed along the edges of the ice pack, cautiously picking her way through the open leads — the channels of water through the ice fields — now toward the east, now the west, hunting for the elusive herds.

Seal hunting was a highly speculative business. If a ship was lucky, she might come back, her hull filled with oil and pelts, and realize huge profits for the cargo in Christiania. If she failed to find the herds before the season ended, she might come home empty-handed, bringing bankruptcy and loss to shipowner and sailor alike.

Each year, in the early spring, the saddleback seals come by the hundreds of thousands to the ice fields around the Jan Mayen Islands, to mate and to bring forth their young. Here the pups, conceived the year before, are born. Plump and fat, they measure about two feet in length and are covered with a soft white downy fleece. It is at this time that they are most sought after, for the pelts of the "whitecoats," as they are called, bring the highest price of all. During this stage they will not go into the water but stay on the ice where they are easy prey for sealers, who kill them by the thousands.

But the weaning season is short; the pups soon lose their soft white coats and take to the water. Then they become wary and alert and must be hunted like the adults, cautiously, from a distance, with long-range rifles.

Back and forth along the edges of the icy fields the *Viking* searched, day after day but without success. Outlooks were posted in the crow's nest twenty-four hours a day, scanning the horizon with powerful telescopes. Conferences were held among the captains of the various ships. Some felt the breeding grounds would be found to the east, others suggested searching toward the west. Route after route was tried only to end in failure. An occasional seal was seen sunning itself on the ice, and in a few cases even groups were sighted. But the crowded, populous rookeries on which the seal hunters depended for a living could not be found. Worst of all, the season for whitecoats was rapidly coming to an end.

One afternoon, in the course of this intensive search, Fridtjof spotted a ship to the leeward. As she drew closer, she appeared strangely different from the others. He noticed her slender rigging with its high double topsails and her smooth graceful lines.

"It's the *Vega*," said one of the sailors.

"Aye," said another. "A fine ship, that. She's done a bit of sailing in her time."

Fridtjof's eyes followed the stately ship with reverence as it moved slowly across the *Viking*'s beam. He had often read about the famous *Vega* and her part in the discovery of the Northeast Passage. Now, he was thinking of all the history she had made, the thousands of miles she had sailed through unknown seas with the celebrated explorer Baron Nils Adolph Erik Nordenskjöld at her helm. It was a sight he was not soon to forget.

Once again, in company with a number of other vessels, the *Viking* headed north, ramming her way through the ice in quest of her elusive prey. Finally, on April 23, the lookout gave the alert. He had spotted a rookery 12 miles off the port bow where thousands of fat, sleek, full-grown seals were scattered about on the ice floes, sleeping in the bright sunshine.

Now, there was a rush of excitement on board as the men climbed up out of the hatches and slid down the rigging. Gunners loaded their weapons, and skinners wrapped around their waists coils of rope hung with skinning knives and sharpening steels.

The boats were lowered away, Fridtjof going along in one as an oarsman. They had barely touched the water when they shoved off, the gunners crouching in the bow directing the steersman. Gliding along silently, taking advantage of every projection, every bit of cover, they worked their way closer to the sleeping seals. Occasionally, a lone bull sentinel in the middle of the herd would raise its head, sniffing the air, searching the surrounding floes for signs of danger.

The boats were closing in now, the men speaking in whispers, hardly daring to breathe. One wrong move could alert the herd and send it scampering over the ice into the water. Carefully, the oarsmen dipped their oars as the ring of boats converged on the sleeping seals. The long seconds ticked by, and to Fridtjof the waiting seemed like an eternity. Then suddenly, at less than a hundred yards, the gunners opened fire, the sharp reports echoing in the brisk morning air.

All around the edges of the floes the big seals shuddered, relaxed and lay still as the speeding bullets found their mark. As long as the gunners hit the brain, killing the animals instantly and cleanly, the remainder of the herd paid little heed to the disturbance. But let a single beast be wounded to thrash about on the ice, and the entire herd would take flight, disappearing into the safety of the sea.

For almost an hour the firing continued until enough

animals were killed to fill the boats. Then the oarsmen jumped out onto the ice to begin the bloody task of skinning. Fridtjof mastered the trade quickly, learning to make a sharp clean cut down the belly, peeling off the skin, taking only the thick yellowish blubber and the pelt, leaving the rest for the birds and scavengers. Even now, as he worked, hundreds of gulls and fulmars descended on the scene, screaming, tugging, fighting greedily over the bloody remains.

As soon as the boats were loaded, they headed back to the ship, where the skins were hoisted aboard. There they were scraped clean of fat, salted down and stored in the curing bins. The thick layers of blubber were later cut into strips to be rendered and boiled down for oil. It was long, hard work, and Fridtjof toiled right along with the crew, skinning, flensing, salting down, doing his share of the work like an old hand.

Seal skinning on the floes

The men had long forgotten that he was only a boy, a university lad, and they accepted him as one of their own. He ate with them, worked with them, sat in the fo'c'sle and listened to their yarns, even entered into their rough-and-tumble games like wrestling and tug-of-war.

Another diversion was target shooting, and there was keen competition among the gunners. Fridtjof prided himself on his marksmanship, and one day Hans, the ship's carpenter, challenged him to a test of skill.

"A quid of tobacco says you can't hit this cartridge," said Hans.

Fridtjof examined the object, a large brass casing. He had often hit targets a good deal smaller than that and at greater distances, so with a confident shrug of his shoulders he accepted.

Hans fastened the cartridge to the ship's railing up near the bow and handed Fridtjof a rifle, a wily grin on his old weather-beaten face.

Fridtjof took his stand, and the crew moved back to give him room. Carefully, he aimed, peering steadily through the sights. Fifty feet away the big cartridge stood out large and clear like a tin can on a backyard fence. Calmly, Fridtjof squeezed the trigger. The rifle barked, followed by a resounding echo. For a long moment there was complete silence. Then suddenly the crew broke out in wild howls of laughter. The big cartridge sat on the railing completely untouched. Fridtjof could hardly believe his eyes.

Hans roared with delight, slapping his fat sides. "What happened, Fridtjof, did the ship move?"

Determined to prove his skill, Fridtjof demanded another chance. "Make it a half-pound of tobacco this time," he said.

"You're on," said Hans, shaking with laughter.

Once again, Fridtjof aimed the rifle. There was no mistaking it this time, the cartridge stood out plain as day against the background of the white ice fields. Patiently, he waited for the wind to die down, then squeezed the trigger. This time he knew he couldn't miss. The rifle cracked, but even before the echo died away the men were doubled over with laughter. The cartridge was still standing, not a mark on it.

Bewildered and frustrated, Fridtjof shook his head. Never in his life had he missed such an easy mark. The men were amused at his bewilderment, Hans laughing hardest of all.

Fridtjof went over to the target, inspecting it carefully for scratches or nicks. Then he glanced down at the rifle, and as he did so he saw the reason for his failure. The rear sight was askew, slightly off-center as though it had been tampered with, and Fridtjof was certain he knew who the culprit was. With a quick motion of his thumb he pushed the sight back to its proper position.

"Give me another chance," said Fridtjof. "And let's raise the stakes to a full pound of tobacco."

"Good as done," said Hans. "You'll be keeping me in smoking tobacco for a month."

Casually, Fridtjof took up his stand a few feet farther away than before. A solemn hush came over the group as he raised the gun to his shoulder. They could sense a difference in his manner. Fridtjof aimed carefully, steadying the rifle on the target, then with perfect precision he fired three shots in quick sucession. The first one clipped the top clean off the cartridge, the second split it neatly down the middle, the third sent it spinning through the air.

The crew gasped in surprise, and now it was Hans's turn to be baffled.

"Set up another one," said Fridtjof. "We'll make it two pounds even."

Hans threw up his hands in defeat. "You win," he said. "One pound is all I can afford."

Fridtjof refrained from disclosing Hans's little secret. A pound of tobacco, he reasoned, was penalty enough.

A short while later, Captain Krefting approached Fridtjof on the half deck. "I hear you're quite a man with a rifle."

Fridtjof smiled. "Hunting rabbits and ptarmigan is pretty good experience," he said. "I've been doing it ever since I was a kid."

"We could use another good marksman in the boats," Krefting said.

The smile on Fridtjof's face spread from ear to ear. "You mean I can take over as a gunner?"

"Boat number seven's open," said Krefting. "She's all yours if you want her, complete with crew."

So Fridtjof became a gunner, riding in the bow of the longboat, directing his men, leading them to the quarry. Within a matter of weeks, he became an experienced seal hunter, his boat coming in day after day piled high with pelts and blubber. He competed on an equal footing with the other gunners, those old veterans of the Arctic, rivalling them in endurance and ability, frequently beating them at their own game. The crew began to look up to him, obeying his commands and respecting his decisions; and in the process, Nansen became a leader of men.

For weeks, they ranged the ice fields, loading the *Viking* down with furs and oil, the plunder of the North. Fridtjof loved the excitement and the activity, but he did not delude himself into believing it was anything except what it really was, a cruel, bloody business. "It was not," he later wrote, "a trade that had any ennobling influence on the emotions of man."

But Fridtjof did not confine himself to the killing of seals. In between hunts there was ample time for the pursuit of his scientific studies, and he followed them with diligence and purpose. He not only skinned the seals, he virtually dissected them, studying their anatomy, examining their stomachs to find out what they had been eating. He measured them, took their temperatures, recorded their weights and made attempts to determine their migrations.

Each day he noted the direction of the winds and the waves. He lowered his thermometers over the side, recording the temperature of the water at various depths. He calculated the movements of the ice, its thickness and consistency, and classified the many forms it took under pressure and erosion.

With rifle and shotgun, he made a collection of Arctic bird life, the gulls, fulmars, auks, gyrfalcons, dovekites, guillemots and many others. With his dip nets he probed the depths of the icy seas, bringing up crustacea, mollusks, fish and other forms of marine life. With his hand lens he studied the plankton, the one-celled plant and animal life that lives suspended in the water or collects in the form of a reddish film on the undersurface of the floating ice. He was busy every minute of the day, never idle, never at a loss for something to do. Frequently, the crew watched him as he worked, some of them lending a hand with his nets and dredges, others wondering what it was all about.

Once, one of them asked the captain what Fridtjof was studying to be.

"He's going to be a naturalist," said Krefting.

The old salt scratched his head. "A naturalist, and

who's going to pay him for that?"

For answer, the captain merely shrugged his shoulders.

"He'd be better off being a vet," said the sailor.

"Why a vet?"

"Because he's a pretty good hand at cutting things up."

Undaunted, Fridtjof went on with his work. He filled his sketchbook with animated drawings of whales, seals and birds. He sketched the men as they went about their work, sailing the ship, hunting seals or scraping down the pelts. He did portraits of Krefting and other members of the crew and innumerable drawings of the *Viking*. He spent long, cold hours perched in the crow's nest sketching the surrounding ice fields, the jagged ridges, the narrow, meandering leads.

And through it all he was learning to know the Arctic, its life, its moods, its very personality. There was something about this grim, white land that fascinated him and made him want to come back. It was to become his lodestone, his guiding star, inevitably leading him on.

Plunder of the North

FOR OVER A MONTH, the *Viking* cruised the ice fields in and around the Jan Mayen Islands, filling her hold with pelts and oil. But the rookeries were thinning out as the season came to an end and the saddlebacks left the breeding grounds.

Now, with the rest of the sealing fleet, the *Viking* turned south in search of larger prey. As she made her way through the warm spring waters of the Denmark Straits, Fridtjof whiled away the hours watching the many whales and dolphins migrating to the northern feeding grounds. He saw large schools of bottle-nosed whales swimming close to, under the bow of the ship, cavorting and rolling about, looking up at him with their dark little eyes alert and curious. He saw the long, slender fin whales and the fat, barrel-shaped humpbacks; and on one occasion he spotted a rare Greenland whale

Male of the bladdernose seal

as it rolled to the surface blowing and showing its flukes.

"If we had that fellow on board," said Krefting, "the voyage would be paid for a dozen times over."

But the *Viking* was not looking for whales. She was searching now for the giant hooded seals or "bladdernoses" as the hunters called them. They were larger than the saddlebacks, reaching a length of ten feet. In the early summer, they gathered by the thousands on the drifting ice floes along the east coast of Greenland, mating, bringing forth their young and feeding on the endless supply of bottom fish. Unlike the saddlebacks, they were inclined to be vicious and aggressive, and the hunters had to be quick to keep out of their way.

A few days later, as the *Viking* picked her way through the open leads, the lookout spotted scattered black dots lying on the ice eight to ten miles away. Hurriedly, boxes of rye biscuits and pork were loaded into the longboats. The men donned their heavy weather gear, the skinners began honing knives while the gunners cleaned their weapons and drew ammunition. Two hours later, the boats were ready, and Krefting gave the command to lower away.

Fridtjof's boat hit the water with a splash and headed for the nearest open lead. The brawny men strained at the oars, and the boat fairly leaped across the waves.

Fridtjof knew there was no need for concealment now, no need for silence. The bladdernose is an inquisitive beast with rather poor eyesight, and at the first sign of danger it will lift itself high on its flippers, searching about for the enemy. In this awkward and exposed position it makes an excellent target.

Standing in the bow, Fridtjof braced himself against the wind, while directly in front of him, only 150 yards away, lay a large bull seal sleeping soundly on the ice. Slowly, they moved in, Fridtjof directing the boat through the open leads. As the range closed, the oarsmen gave one last heave, then shipped oars, letting the boat glide along silently under its own momentum, the steersman keeping it on a steady keel. Fridtjof gave the signal, and with one voice the entire crew began to shout. Instantly, the bull was up, pushing itself high on its front flippers, sniffing the air. He was a huge, ashen-grey beast, with large black spots scattered over his body. He came up with a bellowing roar, the hood, or bladder, over his ugly snout inflating with air.

Fridtjof raised his rifle, sighting carefully, waiting for the range to close. At 80 yards he fired, the blast shattering the cold silence. With a heavy thud, the bull's head dropped to the ice and lay still.

Now, the longboats were moving in from all sides, the guns blazing right and left. The skinners jumped out to begin the bloody task of removing the skins and blubber. It was difficult work, with some of the big bulls weighing up to 800 pounds. Hour after hour, the work continued, the boats plying between the rookery and the ship to unload their cargo.

Gathering around great flaming fires of burning blubber, the men took turns eating their rye biscuits and salt pork washed down with tumblers of beer. Then back to work again, dragging the heavy sealskins across the ice, two or three men hauling at the end of a rope. The slaughter went on, day after day, until the rookery was cleaned out or the remainder of the herd escaped into the safety of the open sea. Only then did the boats make their final run back to the ship.

Fridtjof stood in the bow, his boat riding low in the water. He glanced back at the tired, bone-weary men. It had been almost three days since they left the deck of the *Viking*. And now they would be glad for a hot meal, a warm, dry bunk and a few hours of sleep. Krefting was right, this was nothing but a cold-hearted, dirty business, motivated by a thoughtless desire for money and profits. He was thinking of all this now as he watched the men pulling languidly at the oars. Then, suddenly, he was shaken out of his thoughts by the steersman, who shouted, "Look out ahead."

He spun around in time to see the huge head of an enraged bull seal coming directly for the boat. Quickly, he fumbled for his rifle, but his thick woollen mittens hampered his movements, and he was forced to fire without aiming. The shot missed completely, and a moment later the great bull hurled itself out of the water. It clambered up on the bow, its savage teeth snapping wildly, barely inches from Fridtjof's face. Grabbing up a handy seal club, he struck the beast across the face, knocking it back into the water. In an instant, it was up again, charging from the opposite direction. This time Fridtjof was ready. He fired point-blank into the creature's gaping jaws. It floundered back into the water with a gurgling roar, and the weary sailors watched as its huge body sank slowly into the blue-green depths.

Week after week, the hunt continued, and by the end of the season the *Viking* rode hull down, heavy with the riches of the North.

During the rare intervals of inactivity, Fridtjof continued with his scientific investigations. He made a special study of the big Greenland sharks, huge monsters up to 20 feet long that hung about the ship waiting for scraps of blubber and refuse. With the help of willing crew members, he hoisted them up onto the ice, studying their feeding habits and anatomy. In the stomach of one large specimen, he found two baby seals that had been swallowed intact, and in another a big halibut weighing over 52 pounds. In all, he brought up scores of the huge brutes, cutting out their livers, from which was extracted large quantities of a high-grade train oil.

On June 27, while cruising in the Denmark Straits, the *Viking* sailed into a thick area of rolling fog. Unable to take bearings, she drifted slowly along with the prevailing currents and a few days later found herself helplessly trapped in the ice. It was a condition that Krefting had hoped to avoid but one that was all too common in these northern latitudes. There was nothing to do now but wait and hope the ice would open sufficiently to let the *Viking* free.

Here in the Arctic, one of Fridtjof's primary ambitions was to come face to face with that giant predator of the North, the polar bear. So far during the expedition, there had been a number of sightings, but in every case the animal was too far away to be followed.

Now, one morning as the *Viking* lay trapped in the ice, he was awakened by the mate, who told him there was a bear out on the ice not far from the ship. Quickly, Fridtjof pulled on his clothes and ran up on deck, a rifle in his hand. But before he could get into position another member of the crew fired a shot, frightening the animal away. Instead of giving chase, Fridtjof resorted to a ruse. He placed a huge chunk of salt pork into a frying pan and began cooking it up on deck where the tempting smell would be carried by the wind over the ice. The trick worked, for within a few minutes the bear was back, eagerly sniffing the air, ambling about in a wide circle. Cautiously, Fridtjof started out, dodging from hummock to hummock. He stopped behind a low ridge, waiting for the bear to come within range.

In a slow, steady gait, the hungry animal came closer. It was barely 20 yards away when it spied Fridtjof hiding behind the ridge. It stopped for a moment, undecided, then climbed up on a hummock to get a better view.

As the bear showed itself atop the mound of ice, Fridtjof threw his rifle to his shoulder and pulled the trigger. With a sickening feeling in the pit of his stomach he heard the dull metallic click as the gun misfired. At the same time, the angry bear lunged forward, shuffling across the ice with a menacing growl. Desperately, Fridtjof tried to clear the jammed weapon, but the frozen cartridge refused to budge. Out of the corner of his eye, he saw the bear still coming on with giant, lumbering strides. Again and again, he tried to eject the shell, splitting his nails in the attempt, but the stubborn casing was solidly frozen in the breech.

Quickly he looked around, searching for some means of escape, knowing full well that he was much too far from the ship to expect help from that direction. He would have to make a run for it or stand and fight, using his rifle as a club. Either way, he had little doubt as to the final outcome. In the meantime, the anxious seconds were ticking by, and the bear was almost on him.

With one last effort, he tugged at the cartridge and felt it budge. He yanked again and this time the shell came loose just as the bear loomed over him like a great white shadow. Quickly, he slammed another round into the breech, raised the gun and fired. The bear stumbled and went down, but only for a moment. With a clumsy effort, it got to its feet and in bewildered rage staggered off across the ice.

Fridtjof followed for another mile until the wounded beast reached the edge of an open lead and took to the water. The young hunter waited patiently for the animal to reappear, and in a few minutes it surfaced on the opposite side. The bear climbed up onto the ice, and Fridtjof finished it off with a well-placed shot through the heart. Tired and out of breath, he looked down at the magnificent beast with a mixed feeling of pride and regret. He had shot his first polar bear, but he was to shoot a great many more during his long career.

One of the most exciting encounters of all occurred only a few days later. The lookout had spotted a large bear prowling about, some distance from the ship. When Fridtjof got the word, he bounded up out of the cabin in hot pursuit. After a few miles of tracking, he realized the bear was gaining rapidly by swimming across the areas of open water while he, Fridtjof, had to go around. He reasoned that if the bear could do it, so could he, and he dived in, clothes and all, and paddled for the opposite side. Panting and sputtering, he climbed out, checked his rifle and continued on, icy water sloshing in his shoes. By repeating this procedure a number of times he managed to get within a hundred yards of the startled animal. He was almost on it when it disappeared mysteriously behind a low ridge of ice.

Baffled, Fridtjof searched the area, but the bear was not to be found. Then, standing on the edge of an open lead, he spied the enormous white shadow as it moved quietly through the deep water. Quickly, he jumped aboard a small raft of ice and began paddling across. He had almost reached the middle when suddenly the big bear lunged up with a tremendous roar and threw itself against the ice floe, trying to topple Fridtjof into the water. Tottering about like a tightrope walker, Fridtjof struggled to maintain his balance while trying to get his gun into position for a shot. For a few desperate moments it was touch and go as the enraged animal continued to claw and swipe at the pitching floe. Then, with unsteady aim, Fridtjof managed to get off a lucky shot into the animal's chest. Slowly, the great body began to sink, and Fridtjof was forced to reach down and grab it by the ears, holding on doggedly until Krefting and some of the crew members came up to help him haul it out onto the ice. It was a fine specimen and turned out to be one of the largest bears they had bagged so far.

Krefting looked at Fridtjof standing soaking wet, his blond hair still dripping. "That was a fool thing to do," he said. "If you had fallen into the water that animal would have made short work of you."

For reply, Fridtjof merely stood there, grinning from ear to ear.

"Now get back to the ship with you," said Krefting. "And change into some dry clothes."

With a light heart, Fridtjof started off, leaving the others to take care of the trophy. He had only gone a short distance when he came across a second hunting

An enemy of the bladdernose

party following a bear they had just wounded. Not wishing to interfere, he stepped off to one side and watched the proceedings. The bear circled aimlessly for a few moments. Then, without warning, it suddenly started in his direction. It came on in a wild, loping gait, growling savagely. Fridtjof waited till it came within 20 feet, then he fired. The bear staggered on and fell barely two yards from where he stood.

Once again, Fridtjof started back for the ship, and as he came within sight of the vessel he saw a third bear feeding on the carcass of a dead seal. He chased the animal for over an hour before he finally brought it down. By then it was growing late and he was five miles away from the *Viking*, not even certain of his directions. He fired a signal shot with his last cartridge, and luckily one of his shipmates found him a few minutes later. Together, they skinned the bear and started dragging the heavy pelt back to the ship. Halfway there, they were met by a group of sailors who had been sent out by Krefting to bring them food and drink.

Two hours later, when Fridtjof got back to the ship, Krefting greeted him with a frown. "I expect you're right proud of yourself," he said. "Wet to the skin, running all over the Arctic as though it were some kind of a playing field. If you had been killed or lost, I would have had a great deal of explaining to do back in Christiania."

Fridtjof shifted uneasily. He had had a wild, exciting day, and in spite of his fatigue he was not apt to be discouraged by mere words. Besides, he caught the glint of a smile in Krefting's eyes as he ordered, "Now go below and get out of those wet clothes before you freeze to death."

For twenty-four days the *Viking* drifted along the coast of Greenland, securely locked in the great mass of ice. On clear days they could plainly see the rugged icebound coast, and Fridtjof spent many hours in the crow's nest viewing it through the telescope. He was fascinated by the great shimmering glaciers as they pushed their towering ice-blue walls down to the very edge of the sea.

Here was an exciting land of mystery, an island continent totally unexplored. He wondered what lay beyond those frozen ramparts, those ragged mountains. Was it only an empty wasteland of ice and snow, or did warm fertile valleys and unseen green hills lay hidden beyond that forbidden façade? The very thought made his heart beat faster, challenging him to find out. At one point, when they were only 25 miles from land, he asked Krefting for permission to go ashore, but the captain refused. With the unpredictable fog and the shifting currents, the risk was too great. Fridtjof would have to be content with viewing Greenland through the telescope or reproducing its glacial beauty on his sketch pad.

A few days later, the ice began to break up, and the *Viking* freed herself from the trap, fighting her way out into the open sea. It was like a sudden release after a long term of imprisonment.

The weather was warm and balmy, and with a successful season behind him Krefting plotted a course for home. Ten days later they sighted the pine-covered shores of Norway, and that evening the *Viking* dropped anchor in her home port of Arendal.

Fridtjof Nansen's first expedition was over. Six months of voyaging along the fringes of a new and unknown land had come to an end. He had gone away a boy and on July 27, 1882, had come home a leader of men. One day, in the not-too-distant future, he would go back to that dazzling land of ice and snow, to the graceful ivory gulls and the roaring ice pack. He would go back to write his name in glory, to win fame and worldly acclaim. But for now, he was glad to be home.

Home is the Sailor

WORD OF FRIDTJOF's homecoming travelled fast and his father and Professor Collett, his zoology teacher, came up to Arendal to greet him. Fridtjof rowed ashore in the dinghy. He came striding down the wharf, windburned and tan, towering over his father, taking the old man in his arms in a great bear hug.

His father looked up at him, a mist of tears clouding his tired eyes. "It's good to have you home."

Fridtjof smiled. "It's good to be back."

They talked for a few minutes about the trip, about Fridtjof's health and his future. Professor Collett asked, "And what do you plan to do now?"

Fridtjof was thoughtful for a moment; then he said, "I'll go on with my studies, I suppose."

"There's a position open as curator of zoology at the Bergen Museum," Collett suggested. "You've been recommended for the post."

Fridtjof was surprised. Here he was, barely out of his teens, being offered a position of trust and responsibility. He had just begun his studies in zoology, but this was a golden opportunity to go on into even more stimulating fields of research.

"You'd be working under Dr. Daniel Danielssen," said Collett. "He's a stern taskmaster but a brilliant scientist. You'll learn more zoology from him than you will from anyone else."

It sounded like an interesting challenge, and Fridtjof decided to accept.

For six long years, father and son were separated now by the width of Norway, the father still residing in Christiania. But they managed to keep in touch through frequent correspondence.

In one of his many letters, his father wrote:

Our paths are now almost completely sundered and the long days seem terribly empty for an old man. I must console myself as I did when you were away in the Arctic. People who know about these things tell me that this new post will be of immense value to your career and will enormously facilitate your studies. If this is so, then I am more than happy for you and will bear the loneliness with fortitude.

On his first Christmas away from home, Fridtjof thought of the happy childhood days he had spent at Great Fröen — the vivid memories of his father trimming the big Christmas tree while the children waited impatiently behind closed doors. His thoughts were bathed in the happy glow that surrounds a happy and peaceful home.

To overcome his homesickness, Fridtjof threw himself into his work with energy and purpose, studying, dissecting, classifying. His small laboratory reeked with preservatives while collections of crustacea, gastropods, hagfishes and tunicates cluttered his worktable.

The country around Bergen was damp, the sky frequently overcast. The surrounding hills were covered with a thick, luxuriant vegetation, its brilliance subdued by a persistent, grey, misty drizzle. Occupied with his work, and with little chance for outdoor activity, Fridtjof frequently became depressed with the drab sameness of his circumstances. He longed for the open, sun-filled valleys of Christiania, the deep green mountains and pine forests that he had enjoyed so much as a boy. His heart yearned to escape, to get out into the wilderness again where his spirit was free to roam.

He loved the study of living things, and he was fascinated by the order and logic of science. Yet there was one thing he loved even more, and that was the wild untamed beauty of the great outdoors. By vocation and choice he was a scientist, by nature and inclination he was an explorer, eager to wander across the face of the earth. He was more at home in the deep silence of the untrod wilderness than he was on a city street, more at ease clinging to the peak of a snow-capped mountain than he was at an impressive scientific gathering.

All his life he was to be lured away by this persistent urge, and now each time the impulse came upon him he turned back to his work with renewed zeal.

In letters, his father warned him not to neglect his health, advising him to exercise in the local gymnasium to make up for his lack of physical activity. One day, his father appeared at the laboratory and presented Fridtjof with a heavy package wrapped in stiff, brown paper. "Just a small gift from an old father," he said.

Fridtjof stood there, startled, holding the package in his hands.

Norwegian fjord. This is the type of country Nansen travelled through on his way from Bergen to Christiania.

"Go ahead, open it," said his father.

Clumsily Fridtjof's big fingers undid the wrappings, letting them fall to the floor, revealing a brand-new, shiny, black microscope with bright silver fittings. He stared at it in surprise, stunned by its beauty and workmanship. Carefully, he peered through the wide barrel, his fingers testing the adjusting screw. He turned to his father, his eyes glowing with pride. "It's beautiful, Papa, really beautiful."

The old man held up a restraining hand. "Nonsense, it's just a little thing. I don't know very much about this work of yours, but if you are to succeed you must have the best tools available."

Fridtjof held up the instrument as if it were a precious jewel. He remembered the skis he had received from Mr. Fabritius when he was only a boy. Here again was a chance to explore a new field, an exciting adventure into an unknown world.

As the years passed, Fridtjof's thoughts continued to turn back to the vast unexplored regions of the Arctic. In 1884, he had read the astounding news of Nordenskjöld's attempt to cross Greenland, of how he had plunged almost 80 miles into that vast, frozen wasteland before he had to turn back. It sent Fridtjof's imagination soaring, rousing his spirit with a new yearning for adventure. He was confident that with an experienced team of skiers he could cross that unknown island continent. But now his father was not well, and it would be thoughtless to go barging off into the void, adding another worry to the old man's troubles.

Fighting against this disquieting impulse, he turned back to his studies, spending long hours at his laboratory bench. Using his new microscope and staining his specimens with aniline dyes, he succeeded in tracing the nerve tissue and tangled nerve endings of countless tiny marine invertebrates. All day and far into the night, he dissected and sketched, outlining the complicated patterns of cells and connective tissue. It was tedious, eye-straining work, but he forced himself to keep at it.

But even this was not enough. A few months later, he was off to Italy to learn the new chromic silver method of staining, developed by Professor Camilo Golgi at the university in Pavia, then on to the famous Zoological Station at Naples for further study. He was a bear for activity, filled with unbridled, pent-up energy, the exuberance of youth. At night, in the beautiful, gay city of Naples he went promenading through the Villa Nazionale, with its long rows of stately palms. He took joyous moonlight excursions to Capri and Sorrento, where he danced with the ladies and serenaded the stars. It was a much-needed rest after long years of routine and confinement.

But the rest was soon over, and once again he was back in Bergen, delving into the embryology of whales and working on a thesis for his doctor's degree, entitled, "The Correlation of the Nerve Elements in Marine Invertebrates." It meant another two years of intense, concentrated work, poring over his microscope, and filling thick notebooks with page after page of complicated, diagrammatic sketches and descriptions. The long years passed slowly, and under the stern tutelage of old Dr. Danielssen, Fridtjof became an accomplished scientist.

Then suddenly his old father died, and there was no longer any reason for delaying his return to the Arctic. On a cold winter evening in 1887, Nansen barged into the room of his good friend Dr. Lorentz Grieg and announced that he was going to have a try at crossing Greenland. He said it as casually as if he were going down to the corner grocery store to buy a loaf of bread. With the help of an old atlas, he showed Grieg where he planned to go ashore and how he hoped to fight his way across to the west coast.

Grieg listened patiently. He was used to Nansen's outbursts of optimism, but this time he sensed a deeper, stronger resolution. They went out to a small café, where Fridtjof went on outlining his plans until the small hours of the morning. "I know I'm right," he said. "I can feel it in my bones, but I still want to get an expert's opinion. For that I'll have to go to Stockholm."

"Why Stockholm?" asked Grieg.

"To find Baron Nordenskjöld and ask him what he thinks, then I'll be sure."

The Arctic Calls Again

PROFESSOR W. C. BROGGER hunched over his laboratory bench at the Mineralogical Institute in Stockholm. A heavy ledger lay open before him, and in a firm, neat hand he filled in the date, November 3, 1887. He proceeded to enter a column of figures, copying from a tray of shale specimens on the bench beside him.

As he worked, an old janitor shuffled in with a broom and pail. He set the pail down quietly in the corner of the room, then looked over at the professor. "There's a young feller waiting outside to see you," he said.

Brogger continued with his writing without looking up. "What does he want?"

The janitor shrugged. "I don't know. I think he's Norwegian, maybe a fisherman or a sailor."

"Is he well dressed?"

"Well, he hasn't got an overcoat," said the old man.

"He's pretty tall and he's fair, but he hasn't got an overcoat."

That would be it, thought Brogger, a sailor down on his luck, without an overcoat . . . probably wants to borrow some money. "He'll just have to wait," said Brogger. "I want to get this out of the way first."

The janitor finished his sweeping and went away while Brogger continued his work.

An hour later, one of Brogger's assistants came in, rubbing his hands against the autumn chill. "Have you seen Nansen?" he asked.

"Is that the name of the sailor waiting outside?"

"Yes," said the assistant. "He's a fascinating fellow. I've been talking with him for quite some time. He's going to cross the Greenland ice cap on skis, and he's studying the embryology of whales. He's really quite a remarkable person."

Brogger looked up for the first time. "He's going to do what?"

"He's going to cross the Greenland ice cap," the assistant repeated. "And, by golly, I believe he's just the fellow that can do it."

Slowly, Professor Brogger closed his ledger, at the same time scratching his cheek thoughtfully with the end of his penholder. "Maybe we should have a talk with this sailor," he mumbled. "Maybe we should find out what he's up to." He nodded to his assistant. "Better show him in."

A moment later, Fridtjof came through the door. He walked with great strides, sturdy and erect, moving with the grace of a wild animal. He had a large bushy moustache as blond as the hair on his head. He made straight for Brogger, holding out his hand, not at all perturbed at having been kept waiting. After introducing himself, he said, "Professor Mohn tells me you are a good friend of Baron Nordenskjöld. I thought perhaps you would be kind enough to introduce me."

Brogger ignored the reference to Nordenskjöld and got right to the point. "So you're going to cross Greenland?"

"Yes," said Nansen. "I'm seriously thinking about it."

"Well, if you value your life, you'll stop thinking about it and go do something else. It's impossible."

Nansen's unruffled expression never changed. He was used to people telling him it was impossible. "I don't think it is," he said. "A good team of skiers travelling lightly ought to be able to make the trip in a little less than a month."

Brogger looked into the blue-grey eyes, trying to see beyond the brash recklessness of this impetuous youth. "A month?" he said. "More likely it will take over six months. Have you ever been to Greenland?"

"No, but I've seen it. I sailed along the coast aboard a sealing vessel a few years ago."

"Seeing it and crossing it are two different things. It's the most inhospitable country in the world, covered with snow and ice from shore to shore; freezing winds in the winter, rain, fog and sleet in the summer. It's the worst spot in the entire Arctic, I tell you."

"Nordenskjöld tried it," said Nansen. "So did Peary. I know they didn't make it, but they both came back alive. I still think it can be done."

Brogger threw up his hands in a gesture of frustration. "Certainly Nordenskjöld tried it. He knows the country. Who would know it better? He travelled 80 miles across that ice cap and then had to turn back."

"But his Lapp guides went farther," said Nansen. "They reported snowfields as far as the eye could see.

On that kind of surface a good ski runner ought to be able to travel fast."

"It's over 700 miles wide in some places. You talk as if it were a Sunday picnic. What makes you think you can succeed where others have failed?"

"Because I am convinced that with the right kind of equipment and careful planning it can be done."

Brogger was confused. He was beginning to like this obstinate young man. The more obstacles one placed in his path the harder he fought back. But now he was being stubborn, like a thickheaded Norwegian. Something had to be done. Brogger went over to the closet and put on his hat and coat. "Come," he said. "We will go see Nordenskjöld. He will tell you you're a fool."

They made their way down Queen Street, past the busy crowds of Stockholm, walking briskly in the chill morning air. Nansen was lightly dressed in a navy-blue jersey, yet he seemed perfectly warm and comfortable.

They found Baron Nordenskjöld working in his laboratory. He was a massive man with narrow, dark-piercing eyes and a great bristling moustache. Brogger introduced them.

Nordenskjöld was civil but curt. He was up to his ears in work, and he didn't have time for a young curator from Norway no matter what his problems. He continued examining his specimen while the two men stood behind him waiting. After all he was the great Baron Nils Adolf Erik Nordenskjöld, first navigator of the Northeast Passage, cartographer of Spitsbergen, geologist and Arctic explorer, consultant to the king; and he was busy, very busy.

They stood for a few minutes waiting, Nansen smiling. Then Brogger intruded. "We will take just a moment of your time, Baron, just a moment. You see Mr. Nansen here intends to cross the Greenland ice cap and I thought perhaps you might — "

Nordenskjöld held up his hand, turning slowly as though he were not quite sure what he had just heard. He stared at Nansen for a long moment. "Good heavens," he said. "Why didn't you say so? Are you really serious?"

"Well, I'm going to give it a try," said Nansen. "And I'd like to get your opinion on the proper gear and equipment."

Nordenskjöld's frown disappeared. His eyes lit up with enthusiasm. He drew up chairs and bid his guests sit down. "Now tell me," he said. "When do you propose to start? What areas do you plan to explore?"

Brogger was amazed at the reaction. "I was certain you'd think he was mad."

"Nonsense," said Nordenskjöld. "I think it's a splendid idea. I only wish I were young enough to make the trip. Come now, tell me all about it. Who is going with you?"

"I plan to make up a team of four or five expert skiers. We'll go ashore a little above Cape Dan in the vicinity of latitude 66 north and work our way northeast to Christianshaab on Disko Bay."

Nordenskjöld gasped, his eyes widening. "You're going ashore on the east coast? But this is unheard of. What about the ice pack? You'll never get past it."

"I've sailed through the pack," said Nansen. "I know what it's like. If we can get in close enough I believe we can cross it. Once ashore all we have to do is climb up on the glacier and we're on our way."

Brogger sat there, listening, shaking his head in disbelief.

"But even if you do reach shore," warned Nordenskjöld, "you've left yourself no means of escape. You'll be stranded. If you have to retreat you have nothing to come back to, no ship, no port, no settlement, nothing."

"That's exactly the point, don't you see? We'll be burning our bridges behind us. Once we start we'll have to go on no matter what. The west coast and Disko Bay will be our only hope of survival."

"See," said Brogger. "I told you he was mad."

Nansen went on in spite of Brogger's protests. "Of course our main objective is scientific. We'll take meteorological observations at every opportunity — winds, temperature, barometer readings. We'll study the conformation of the ice cap as we go along, noting its texture and configuration."

"Good, good," said Nordenskjöld, forgetting his earlier objections. "And remember, there's a good chance you might find land, outcroppings of rock or mountain ranges. In that case geological observations would be most important."

Nansen nodded in agreement. "Travelling by ski, dragging the sleds behind us, we ought to be able to carry enough supplies for at least two months."

Nordenskjöld was growing more excited by the minute, almost as though it were his own expedition he was planning. "Take plenty of concentrated foods," he said. "They're light, they take up little space and they give lots of energy, stuff like meat powders, chocolate, dried fish and condensed milk."

"And pemmican," said Nansen.

"By all means pemmican. It's the staff of life in the Arctic."

They went on for hours, discussing plans, drawing up lists of supplies, clothing and equipment, Nordenskjöld offering a great deal of advice drawn from his long years of experience.

When they were ready to leave, Nordenskjöld went over to a cabinet and took out a pair of reindeer-skin boots brightly ornamented with intricate beadwork. Without ceremony, he offered them to Nansen.

The youth was speechless. He stood there looking at this great man, hardly knowing what to say.

"Go ahead," said Nordenskjöld. "Take them. They're yours. It's very important to have good footgear when travelling across the ice. It could make the difference between success and failure."

They shook hands in parting, and Nansen said, "You are very generous. I don't know how to thank you."

Nordenskjöld smiled, nodding his great shaggy head. "And remember to wear snow goggles. If you become blind you are as good as lost. Plan meticulously, down to the last detail, and you will have success." He slapped the young man on the back. "Now good luck, and come home safe."

As they started for the door, Brogger hung back, whispering aside to Nordenskjöld. "What do you think?"

The old man smiled, his eyes twinkling with envy. "I wager he'll make it."

"You know something," said Brogger. "I still think he's mad, but I agree with you."

Full of confidence, Fridtjof Nansen returned home to Norway a few days later. He knew now that his idea was sound, for even the great Nordenskjöld had approved of it. He made formal announcement of his plan in the periodical *Naturen* and put in a request to the Norwegian government for a grant of five thousand kroner to outfit and finance the expedition. It was a paltry sum for such an ambitious undertaking, but it was a beginning.

While he waited for his answer, he returned to his post in Bergen, on the coast of Norway, and got back to work on his doctor's thesis. After several weeks that seemed like an eternity, the answer finally came, delivered in a long white envelope bearing the official stamp of the government. He tore open the flap and read the crisp, impersonal message. The harsh, blunt words swam before his eyes, and he felt the bitter pang of disappointment catch in his throat. His request had been denied.

In a rush of indignation, he threw on his jacket, shouldered his skis and barged out into the night. He walked briskly past the old Hansa quay with its grey fishing boats bobbing at their moorings. He continued on along the narrow cobblestone streets, past the rows of high-peaked, slate-roofed houses to the railroad station. From Bergen, he took a train eastward to the small town of Voss, and then went by skis over the mountains to Christiania.

It was January, and bitter winter winds howled through the passes, piling up blankets of snow in the valleys and on the slopes of the rugged peaks. The ponds were frozen over, and the only sign of the meandering streams was the melodic gurgling of water beneath the snow.

At Voss, he strapped on his skis and started overland across the mountains to Christiania, 200 kilometers away. The tall pine forests were still, with only the mournful cry of the wolf to disturb the silence. The air was crisp and clear, and under the dark shadows of the pines the snow lay thick in gentle sweeping drifts.

Hushed, too, was the swishing sound of Nansen's skis as he moved through the trees. Head down, eyes on the trail, he glided along at a rapid rate, careening down the hills, swerving between the spruce trees, skirting the edge of the overhangs.

Day and night he pushed on, struggling up through the steep passes, flying down the slopes on the opposite side. Farmers and mountain people who met him on the way thought he was out of his mind. For only a madman would try such a dangerous journey in the middle of winter.

Two days later, he was making his way through Konsberg, and early the next morning he reached Christiania, where he went directly to the home of Professor Mohn, his guide and mentor.

Mohn came to the door at his knock. He was a small, portly man with wide flaring sideburns and a big, jovial smile. He noticed Nansen's exhausted condition and invited him in. "What in heaven's name is the matter?" he asked. "You look done in."

Ignoring Mohn's concern, Nansen reached into his pocket and pulled out the long white envelope. "Well, I got my answer," he said.

"Your request for funds?"

"Yes, it's been rejected. They're not interested."

"I'm sorry," said Mohn. "But I can't say that I'm surprised."

"But I don't understand it," said Nansen. "I thought they'd be proud to have a Norwegian the first man across Greenland."

Mohn saw the bitter disappointment in his eyes. He tried to comfort him. "Come," he said, "stay for breakfast, we'll talk about it."

But Nansen was silent during the meal, glum and brooding, not his usual buoyant self.

"You know," said Mohn, smiling. "Most people think of you as a scholar, not a sportsman. Yet you continually surprise them by making these long ski jaunts, climbing mountains or running off to sea. They're not used to associating scholastic achievements with athletic prowess, and they find it a bit difficult to understand."

Nansen winced, a pained expression on his boyish face. "Perhaps I ought to make a competition out of it, a snowshoe race across Greenland. Maybe they'd be more willing to accept that."

"I'm afraid they've already done it," said Mohn. He picked up a newspaper and opened it on the table in front of Nansen, jabbing his finger at one of the columns.

Slowly, word by word, Nansen read the piece Mohn referred to: "We see no reason why the Norwegian people should pay so large a sum in order that a private individual might treat himself to a pleasure trip across Greenland."

In still another paper there was a notice with a lighter twist. "In the month of June next Fridtjof Nansen proposes to give a skiing display, with long jumps, across the inland ice of Greenland. Reserve seats may be had in the crevasses. Return tickets not necessary."

Nansen looked up, deeply hurt, shaking his head slowly. "Do you suppose this is how they all feel?"

"No, not all, but enough to count at any rate. They look upon it as some kind of a publicity stunt. Others consider it downright suicide."

Nansen was sitting there, his fists clenched at his sides, his blue-grey eyes staring off into the distance. Suddenly, he got to his feet and began storming about the room. "Well, they're wrong," he shouted. "All of them, they're dead wrong. It's not a stunt, and it's not a suicide mission. It's a well-thought-out, carefully organized expedition." He reached the end of the room and turned about, groping for words. "It's science, that's what it is, a far-reaching scientific venture, important both to Norway and to the progress of Arctic exploration. And I intend to prove it even if I have to raise the money myself."

Mohn eyed him intently, the flicker of a smile crossing his thin lips. Here was the real Fridtjof Nansen, full of life and vitality, ready to defy the world. It was the Nansen he had known for many years, the impetuous youth who was always doing the unexpected, always ready to attempt the impossible. "You don't have to convince me," said Mohn. "You have to convince the people who can give you the money."

"I will," said Nansen. "I'll go to the university and ask the Student Society to raise a subscription." There was a brief silence; then he said, "Of course I'll need a sponsor."

"I've backed you this far," said Mohn. "I might as well go all the way."

"You're a good friend. I owe you more than I can ever repay."

"Nonsense," said Mohn. "I believe in you and what you are trying to do. Your success will be reward enough. Now, give me a few days to get things started. I'll speak to the secretary about having you address the council. Be at my office at noon on Wednesday. Perhaps I'll have word for you by then."

Mohn watched as the young man went down the front steps. He noticed once again the broad shoulders and the wide, confident stride. He knew that if anyone could cross that frozen land of ice, Fridtjof Nansen would be the man.

6

Six Against the North

During the next few days in Christiania, Nansen crammed for his forthcoming exams. It was distracting work, for his mind that spring of 1888 was on the absorbing problem of Greenland. This gigantic island had intrigued the mind of man from the days of the earliest Vikings; time and again adventurers had struck out across its barren wastes only to be turned back by howling winds and subzero temperatures. And now, after all these years, it still remained a cold, massive continent of ice and snow, shrouded in mystery, the true gateway to the North — untouched, uncharted, unknown.

There were a few Danish settlements on the sheltered west coast and small bands of Eskimos eking out a precarious existence along the shoreline. But the long eastern coastline, facing the open Atlantic, was a barren and desolate land. Gigantic glaciers pushed huge fingers of ice down to the sea, forming a nearly impenetrable barrier hundreds of feet high. And even this natural edifice was blocked for miles around by drifting ice floes, a tangled, grinding mass of bergs and pack ice that made direct access all but impossible. As for the interior, that great hinterland was as unknown as the far side of the moon.

Fridtjof Nansen was fully aware of all this. He knew the difficulties that would have to be surmounted, the obstacles that would have to be overcome, yet he was ready to expend every energy, face any hardship to see it through.

On Wednesday at exactly twelve noon, Nansen walked into Mohn's office. The walls of the small room were covered with maps and weather charts, the big mahogany desk piled high with books. Mohn came forward, greeting him with a smile, brimming over with good news.

"You have their consent?" asked Nansen hopefully.

"Better than that." said Mohn. "We just received word through the College Academy that a Mr. Augustin Gamel of Copenhagen has offered to put up the money for your expedition."

Nansen stood with his mouth open, hardly daring to believe what he had just heard.

"Mr. Gamel is a lawyer," Mohn continued, "a patron of the sciences, and of Arctic exploration in particular. He likes the sound of your plan and thinks you have a good chance of success."

There was a long silence while Nansen tried to understand what had happened. "You hesitate," said Mohn. "That's not like you."

"No," said Nansen, quickly. "I accept; of course I accept. But this Mr. Gamel is a complete stranger, yet he has faith in my plan. It's almost like a dream."

"I imagine it is. Especially after the opposition you've had. But that's all behind you. Now you can look ahead."

"Yes, and I've got a lot to do. There's equipment to get ready, provisions to buy, and I still have to stand for my degree."

"It'll be summer then before you can get away?"

"We'll leave Iceland aboard a sealer as soon as the weather breaks, probably sometime in June."

They walked together to the door, Nansen trying to keep the excitement out of his voice. "Thank you," he said. "You've no idea what this means to me."

"Maybe this is only the beginning," said Mohn. "Perhaps someday you'll go to the North Pole and prove my theory about an Arctic current."

Nansen thought for a moment; then he said, "You know, I believe I'd like that. I'd like that just fine."

Now began the long, hectic weeks of preparation, the gathering of equipment, the recruiting of the men who were to make the hazardous journey. Stores of provisions and supplies were ordered, examined and tested: tents, tarpaulins, snowshoes, clothing, footgear; and tools for every purpose and of every description — from geology hammers to darning needles. Only the best, the most durable, were selected and packed for the journey.

Nansen personally designed the all-important sleds and supervised their construction. They were made of ash and maple, all joints lashed tightly together with leather thongs to provide strength and flexibility, the runners sheathed in wide bands of steel to prevent them from sinking into the soft snow. They were surprisingly light and could easily be managed by one man when fully loaded.

In the midst of all this, Nansen found time to complete his thesis and take his degree. It was done casually, almost as an afterthought, as though it were some small task that had to be disposed of.

"I would rather take a bad degree," he said, "than start out on an expedition with a bad outfit." It was the explorer talking, not the scholar.

On the seventeenth of July, 1888, the schooner *Jason* rammed her bow through the loose pack ice off the coast of Greenland, nine miles south of Cape Dan. Around her was a solid expanse of white with open leads running in toward shore. High in the rigging, Fridtjof Nansen trained his field glasses on the distant coastline, searching for a likely path through the ice. For two weeks now, they had been skirting the coast, trying to get in close enough to land. Often the ice pack extended 40 or 50 miles, making a direct landing impossible.

Now they were approximately 2½ miles offshore, as close as they were likely to get. Suddenly, Nansen leaned down, shouting through cupped hands, "Sermilik Fjord in sight."

Down below, a heavyset, bearded man glanced up into the rigging. He stood with his feet planted wide apart like a sailor, his hands on his hips. "Where away?" he shouted back, his voice like gravel in a drum.

"Two points off the starboard bow."

The big man whirled around in the direction indicated and for a long moment studied the horizon. His face was leathery tan with tiny squint creases around the corners of his mild brown eyes. His hair was red to match a fiery, wide-flaring beard. Otto Sverdrup was a retired sailing master. He had run off to sea as a boy, shipping on everything from trawlers to merchantmen, working his way up from deckhand to captain. Like Nansen, he had grown up amid the forests and fjords of Norway, learning to hunt, fish and ski at an early age. When he heard of the expedition to cross Greenland, he

Otto Sverdrup (from a photograph taken in 1895)

volunteered immediately. Nansen met him, took an instant liking to him and appointed him second in command.

Some distance away was a tall young man sitting on a hatch cover, with a large map of Greenland spread out before him. He stood up from time to time sighting through a sextant, taking bearings of the distant horizon.

"Well, Oluf, what do you think?" It was Nansen, who had just come down from the rigging.

Oluf Dietrichson was the expedition's cartographer and meteorologist. A former army lieutenant, he was intelligent, eager and tough as whipcord, exactly the kind of man the expedition needed. He glanced up at Nansen, a broad smile on his young, handsome face. "The wind's just right, Sir. We'll never have a better chance."

"All right, then," said Nansen, "you can start loading your instruments as soon as you're ready."

Next, Nansen went over to a youth who was busy loading one of the whaleboats. His name was Kristian Kristiansen, and he was little more than a boy; but he was strong and willing, and he had pleaded persistently for weeks on end to be taken along on the expedition. Finally Nansen had had to give in.

"Have you written to your parents?"

The youngster looked up, bright eyes shining with anticipation. "Yes, Sir, two letters, one to my mother," then with a bashful grin, "and another to my girl."

"Good," said Nansen, trying to hide a smile. "Give them to Captain Jacobsen. He'll see that they're delivered in Copenhagen along with the others."

The members of the Greenland expedition

The last two members of the expedition, Ole Nielsen Ravna and Samuel Johannesen Balto, both from Lapland, were standing near the starboard rail, gazing out at the inhospitable land. They wore strange, four-cornered hats and loose-fitting tunics with long, wide skirts edged in red and yellow. Their faces were wrinkled and dark with distinct Mongoloid features. The smaller of the two, diminutive in size, pointed out across the sea of ice. "It is an empty land covered with clouds," he said. "This is a bad omen. Maybe we will never come back."

Nansen overheard the disquieting remark and walked up to the two men. "You are wrong, Ravna. It is no different from your own country. Ice and snow, you should be used to that."

"Aye," said the little man. "But Lapland has many reindeer." He waved a hand toward the forbidding-looking coast. "Here is nothing."

Turning to the other man, Nansen said, "There is no need for fear, is there, Balto? It will be just like skiing in Finnmark."

Balto smiled, uncertain. "If Herr Nansen says it will be so, then I am not afraid."

Nansen slapped him on the back. "Come, then, let us help load the boats. There is not much time." He thought it best to keep them busy, to distract their minds from imaginary fears. He had hoped their nomadic life as Laplanders would make them ideal guides and packmen. Instead, he found them timid and apprehensive. He was sorry that he had brought them along, but it was too late to send them back.

The two boats were ready now, and the six men climbed over the side, three into each boat, Sverdrup commanding one, Nansen the other. As they pulled away, a loud cheer went up from the crew of the *Jason*. It was a final good-bye, their last link with civilization.

Ravna looked back, searching for the dim outline of the departing ship, his dark, round face a study of dejection. "This sea will be our grave," he moaned. "I should never have left Lapland."

Nansen paid little heed to his whimperings; he was too busy pushing aside the ice floes, making passageway for the boats. The men strained at the oars, guiding the small craft between the drifting floes.

For fifteen hours they struggled, fighting their way doggedly, pushing, shoving, ramming the boats along, even dragging them over the rough ice. Yet, as the hours passed, they seemed to be making little progress. Tired, wet and hungry and with one boat damaged, they decided to pull the boats up on the ice and camp there for the night.

The following morning, the distant shore seemed farther away than ever, and with a sudden shock Nansen began to realize what had happened. During the night, the tiny ice island on which they were camped had been caught up in the moving current, and now they were being swept along far from their intended destination.

All around them, the churning ice pack groaned and thundered as floe jammed against floe. In this grinding millrace of destruction, the boats would be crushed to matchwood. There was little they could do except stand by helplessly and watch the mountains of Greenland fade away into the distance.

Days went by, days of bitter cold and howling winds, of torrential rains and blinding snow. And all the while they were steadily drifting south, slowly, relentlessly south, past the long, rugged coastline of Greenland, so near and yet so far, like a taunting image in a shadowy dream.

Their course was erratic and unpredictable, now in toward shore, now out toward sea. It was a constant battle of nerves as their tiny ice island was imminently threatened with destruction. All during the day, they watched the pounding breakers dash against the edge of the ice shelf, sending mountains of spray and freezing spindrift into the air. To Nansen it was a magnificent display of unbridled power; to Balto and Ravna it was an ominous prelude to death.

In the face of this danger, they were ever on the alert, and during the long hours of the night they took turns standing watch. On one such occasion Sverdrup had the midnight shift. Calmly, he trudged up and down in the pale moonlight, watching the advancing breakers surge closer and closer. Balto and Ravna were cowering in the bottom of one of the boats, reading their Lapp Bible, preparing for doom. Nansen and the others were sleeping in a nearby tent.

Unruffled, Sverdrup watched as the lashing surf swept across the floating island foaming at the edge of their campsite, threatening to engulf it. He had nerves of steel, this man, his quick brown eyes flashing in the moonlight, defying the sea to do its utmost. Once, twice, the water lapped around the edges of the tent, yet Sverdrup stood his ground, reluctant to wake the sleeping men. Briefly, Nansen was aroused by the noise, but when he heard the sound of Sverdrup's reassuring step he turned over and went back to sleep.

Buffeted by gales, tossed about by raging tides, they continued drifting south, sometimes in sight of land, sometimes far out at sea, surrounded by miles of drifting ice.

But the wind did not always howl nor did the sea always rage. There were days of almost balmy sunshine and nights when a great golden moon came out, bathing the surrounding landscape in a pale luminescent glow, changing the pinnacles of ice into a glistening fairyland

Samuel Johannesen Balto   Ole Nielsen Ravna

and the distant mountains into a soft silhouette of purple hills. It was on such evenings that Nansen got out his drawing materials and sketched the never-ending panorama of Greenland as it passed before their eyes.

Often, Sverdrup stood beside him watching him work. Kindred spirits, they sometimes stood like this for hours, each man enjoying the magnificent solitude of this Arctic wasteland in his own particular way. At other times they sipped steaming cups of black coffee, smoked their pipes and talked in low undertones so as not to wake the others.

When sketching, Nansen worked rapidly, outlining the

rugged mountains with quick, deft strokes, glancing over his shoulder from time to time. "Have you ever seen such wild, savage beauty?" he asked. "Such an ordered confusion of earth and sky."

"It's superb," said Sverdrup. "And those glaciers seem to come right down out of the valleys."

"We've got a front-row seat. No one has ever seen it quite this way before."

"Yes," Sverdrup agreed. "But I'm afraid we're drifting too far south."

"Much too far. If we don't make land soon, we'll drift right around Cape Farewell."

There was a note of disappointment in Sverdrup's voice. "And then it will be too late."

"Perhaps, but there's always another year. We can try again."

"I had no idea the current would be this strong," said Sverdrup. "It's sweeping us along like a river."

"And it originates way up in Siberia," said Nansen. "I daresay if one started at the right spot and followed it along, he could drift directly across the North Pole."

Sverdrup gasped. "You really think it's possible?"

"Professor Mohn does, and from all the evidence I've seen I'm inclined to agree with him." There was a brief silence, then Nansen said, "Someday I'm going to try it."

"It's incredible. You'll be able to camp on the ice, just like this, and reach the North Pole without taking a step."

"Not on the ice," corrected Nansen. "On a ship."

"A ship?"

"Yes, a specially constructed vessel that would rise above the pressure of the ice and drift along with it without being crushed."

Sverdrup's strong white teeth flashed in a grin. "It sounds tremendous."

"Perhaps you'd like to come along?"

"I would, by George, whenever you're ready."

"It will take a few years to get organized, and it will cost a great deal of money. But the scientific work that could be acomplished would be of enormous value. On that basis alone, I ought to be able to get all the support I need."

They discussed the exciting project far into the night, and when they were ready to turn in, Sverdrup said, "You're really serious about this?"

"I am."

"That settles it then, I'm going with you. You won't forget?"

"I promise," said Nansen.

A few days later, their ice island drifted into an extensive area of thick, rolling fog. The sea was calm and everything about them was wrapped in a deathly stillness. All night long they drifted through this curtain of silence. Toward morning, Sverdrup heard the ominous crash of surf, but this time it was coming from the wrong direction. Bewildered and confused, he checked his position repeatedly but always with the same results. According to his compass, the sound was coming from the west.

He waited patiently, pacing back and forth, and then, with the first sign of dawn, the fog began to lift. It revealed a wide expanse of open sea leading directly to land. His compass had been right after all.

Quickly, he aroused the others, and they began to load the boats. By sunup they were straining at the oars, greeted by flocks of Sukas, large grey sea gulls, swooping around their heads. They reached the shore and pulled the boats up on the rocky shingle while Ravna and Balto ran up the mountainside, clutching at handfuls of turf and moss, giggling like happy children, glad to be alive.

7

First Across Greenland

FOR TEN DAYS they had drifted south at the mercy of the winding current, and now they were over 300 miles beyond their appointed destination. The best of the summer was behind them, and only 180 miles away lay Fredriksdal, a small village on the southern tip of Greenland. Here they could find warm food and clothing and a semblance of civilization. Here they could wait out the winter in safety and comfort, perhaps to try again another year.

But Nansen would have none of it; there was still time to recover lost ground, still time to cross the inland ice. He would not give up without a fight.

They turned north once again, working their way up the coast, rowing, paddling, dragging the boats over the ice, passing beautiful fjords, hemmed in by mountains that came right down to the edge of the water. They

Travelling across the inland ice

glided silently through iridescent caverns of ice and sailed past towering glaciers hundreds of feet high, narrowly missing destruction as huge sections toppled into the sea.

They lived on seal meat and sea gulls and occasionally met friendly bands of Eskimos, who helped them on their way. Seven days later, they had travelled some 200 miles and reached Umivik Fjord. Here Nansen stopped to make a survey. The season was growing short now, and he thought it was about time to start their long, arduous trek across the inland ice.

After caching the boats in a deep cleft between the rocks, they loaded the sleds with gear and provisions, then started out single file up the steep incline. Travelling by night, they took advantage of the hard crust formed on the snow by the lower nocturnal temperatures. Slowly, they plodded along, Nansen and Sverdrup pulling the leading sled. As they worked their way upward the going was easy, but soon they came to a wide area of ridges and peaks covered by new snow.

Mile after mile they continued, with Nansen slightly in the lead. Suddenly, the ground dropped out from under his feet, and he felt himself falling through space. He waved his arms wildly, trying to regain his balance, while clouds of powdery snow swirled about him. Deeper and deeper he fell, then with a jarring wrench the leather harness bit into his shoulders, halting his plunge. He dangled for a long moment, swinging back and forth, staring down into the cold, bottomless pit. He shook his head to clear his foggy brain, and slowly he began to realize what had happened. He had broken through a thin crust of snow covering a hidden crevasse. Fortunately, the long sled had become wedged across the chasm, stopping his fall, leaving him hanging at the end of his harness.

A moment later, he heard the anxious voices of Sverdrup and Balto calling down to him. He shouted back to assure them of his safety, then felt himself being hauled slowly to the surface.

"That was a close one," said Sverdrup.

Nansen smiled, brushing himself off. "From now on, we'll use ski poles to probe the way ahead."

In spite of this precaution, almost every member of the expedition had the unpleasant experience of falling through a hidden crevasse.

Often, during the days that followed, they came to deep canyons of ice, too wide to cross, and they were forced to go miles out of their way to find a more passable route. They travelled slowly, sometimes only

"Sailing" on the inland ice

three or four miles a night, five if they were lucky. They fought against biting winds and cold freezing rains, were slowed down by roaring blizzards and stopped short by impassable ravines.

And all the while, Nansen enjoyed the challenge of pitting his strength and stamina against the raging elements. To him cold and fatigue were rigid tests of endurance, and distance a personal adversary to be beaten back and conquered.

At 6,000 feet, Nansen estimated they had reached the crest of the ice cap, yet their path continued upward. Here, the temperatures dropped into the minus forties. Thermometers froze, hands and feet frequently became frostbitten and icy wind penetrated through heavy clothing.

On fair, cloudless nights, the moon came out bright and yellow, lighting their way with a radiant, golden sheen that emblazoned the landscape for miles around.

They had been travelling by night to take advantage of the hard-crusted snow produced by the nocturnal sub-zero temperatures. But now, as they gained altitude the snow retained its hard surface even under the glaring sunlight and they were able to travel by day, traversing a region of enormous snow hills stretching away as far as the eye could see, like a vast desert of soft white dunes. It was exhausting work pulling the sleds up the rise of each hill, then struggling to hold them back as they careened down the opposite slope. Here, too, the blazing sun beat down, burning their faces and blistering their lips. The men covered their heads with bright red veils to protect themselves from its penetrating rays.

Step by step, the altitude increased, and every few hours Nansen called a halt. The explorers sat beside the loaded sleds eating frozen oatmeal biscuits, lentil soup and liver pâté. For drinking water, each man scooped up a small quantity of snow and carried it in a metal flask. This was tucked beneath the clothing to be melted by the heat of the body.

After nearly ten days of weary plodding, Nansen realized they had covered barely one-fifth of the total journey. And now, with the summer almost over, the harsh Arctic winter would soon sweep down on this bleak, desolate land, making further travel impossible. Anxiously, Nansen pondered the situation, and that night, after they made camp, he spoke about it to Sverdrup.

"You're right," said Sverdrup. "At this rate our food supply will give out long before we reach the coast. We might dump some of the equipment and one or two of the sleds. That way we can travel faster."

"Better yet," said Nansen, "we could change our course."

Sverdrup shook his head, puzzled. "But then we wouldn't be heading for Disko Bay."

"Exactly," said Nansen. "If we strike out south southwest, we'll be making directly for Godthaab. That's only 200 miles away."

"And we'd still be crossing the island."

"With luck we ought to make it by the end of September."

Sverdrup grinned, the glint of understanding shining in his eyes. "I think the men would like that."

"Good," said Nansen. "We'll start out first thing in the morning. Let's hope we find a ship in port when we get there."

The next morning, the wind was up, and they set to work lashing the sleds together, improvising sails from the tent canvas and tarpaulins, rigging them with ropes. When they were finished, they had a pair of unwieldy-looking iceboats, one consisting of two sleds, the other of three. Each could be guided by a man on skis steering from the front with the aid of a long bamboo pole. These iceboats were perhaps the most unusual means of transportation in the history of Arctic exploration, but after a few minor accidents and a little practice they performed beautifully.

Perched on the loaded sleds, hanging on by ropes, stays or straps, the explorers went flying over the snow, leaping from crest to crest at incredible speeds, covering tremendous distances in the space of a few short hours. It was an exciting, breathtaking mode of travel, but it lasted only a few days. Then the wind died down, and they were back to snowshoes again, fighting through the deep drifts step by step.

At 8,000 feet, they reached a vast plateau of snow that extended without a break for miles. Day after day for what seemed like an eternity, they trudged across this monotonous landscape, guided only by compass and their own dead reckoning. As week followed week and there was still no end of ice and snow, Nansen became uneasy. According to his calculations, they should soon be in sight of the coast. Yet, as far as he could determine, they were still a long way from their destination.

He said nothing of this to the men, but as they plodded on, mile after weary mile, it gave him cause for concern. It took him back to his childhood on a cold autumn night in the woods around Nordmarka. He was stumbling through the dark pine forest, his brother Alexander by his side, searching for a path that would lead home. They had been gone since early morning, and now it was almost midnight. Never before had they been out so late, and they knew their parents would be worried.

An hour later, tired and hungry, they found their way back, and as they started up the walk Nansen saw his mother waiting for them at the gate. She was a big, strong woman, tolerant but firm, and the boys expected a good, sound thrashing. As they came closer, she moved out of the shadows, planting herself in their path, her arms folded. She shook her head slowly, clicking her tongue.

"What strange boys you are," she said. "Staying out so late without supper. Your father has been looking all over for you. Now get to the kitchen; there's some stew simmering on the stove. Then to bed with you before he comes home."

The two boys ran up the stairs without glancing back, thankful that they had a mother who understood.

Now, marching across this vast wasteland, searching for a tiny village hidden somewhere along a desolate coast, Nansen hoped his luck would hold. Dietrichson took another reading with the theodolite, an instrument used for measuring angles. It showed a slight but definite

FIRST ACROSS GREENLAND

fall in the gradient of the ice. This was a heartening sign, but it wasn't until some days later that Nansen's hopes were fully revived.

He was sipping a cup of coffee, sitting on the edge of the sled when, suddenly, he caught sight of a tiny brown bird hopping about the snow in the bright sunshine. He recognized it at once as a snow bunting, a small sparrowlike bird of the open barrens, a sure sign that the coast was not far away.

Two days later, Balto spotted the first faint line of mountains far off on the western horizon. It gave them a tremendous lift. They were in sight of their destination! For sixty-seven days they had fought, clawed, stumbled and climbed across one of the most formidable regions on earth. They had conquered the ice-bound realm of Greenland. They had done the impossible. Now they stood, staring off into the distance, trying to comprehend this incredible feat.

It was all downhill now, with Nansen leading them on. Dietrichson continued his daily observations, checking

Observation taking and dinner on the inland ice

the slope of the ice with his theodolite, taking bearings, wind velocities and temperatures. From the time they had left the *Jason,* through all the storms and blizzards, in spite of the subzero temperatures and frostbitten fingers, he had never missed a sighting, never overlooked an entry. His notebook was a complete physical account of the journey from coast to coast down to the last mile.

On September 24, 1888, they came to the edge of the ice cap and looked down on a beautiful, clear, freshwater lake surrounded by the first green vegetation they had seen in months. They raced for it and fell to their knees, drinking in the clean, cool water and inhaling the rich, earthy smell of its grassy banks.

Within a few more days, they were at the west coast of Greenland, and after a quick study of the difficult terrain Nansen concluded that the easiest way to reach Godthaab would be by sea. Using the tent canvas as a hull and willow branches for cross-ribs, Sverdrup and Balto set to work constructing a boat. The oars were made of long bamboo poles, the blades fashioned out of forked willow branches covered with cloth. It was a clumsy contraption at best, but Nansen and Sverdrup climbed in and blithely set sail for Godthaab, some 60 miles away. The other members of the expedition set up camp and waited. As soon as Nansen and Sverdrup reached civilization they were to send back a boat to pick them up. In the meantime, the two men paddled along the coast, braving gales and choppy seas and living on sea gulls and pemmican. Six days later, on October 3, they came upon a party of Greenlanders fishing offshore. Within a matter of minutes, their small craft was surrounded by dozens of kayaks with chattering, grinning natives, all eager to guide them to the nearby village of Godthaab. There, they pulled the little canvas boat up on shore, smiling back at the excited Eskimos, who were jabbering in wonder at these strange visitors from out of nowhere.

Suddenly, Sverdrup glanced up and said, "Look, here comes a European."

Sure enough, a tall, blond young man came striding toward them. Dressed in a deerskin jumper with a tam-o'-shanter on his head, he was a strange contrast to the milling crowd of natives. He approached casually, holding out his hand. "Do you speak English?" he asked.

Nansen detected the Danish accent and replied in Norwegian, "No, we are Norwegians."

The young man smiled. "And may I ask your name?"

"My name is Nansen, and we've just come from the interior."

"Ah yes," said the youth, his face lighting up. "Fridtjof Nansen. Allow me to congratulate you on taking your doctor's degree."

Nansen was amused. The situation was ridiculous, and it was all he could do to keep from laughing. He had just travelled hundreds of miles across the uncharted face of the Arctic, accomplishing a feat that no man had ever done before, and here was a proper young Danish official congratulating him on an academic achievement that had taken place almost six months before.

The season was late and there were no longer any ships in Godthaab, but Nansen quickly got off a letter to Augustin Gamel telling him of their success and their safe arrival on the west coast. He sent the message by native kayak to meet the last steamer out of Ivitut, 300 miles away. Next, he made immediate arrangements to have a whaleboat pick up the other four members of the expedition.

Godthaab was little more than a cluster of Eskimo huts, a few European dwellings and a church. Here they spent the winter, hunting, fishing and getting to know the

Godthaab in winter garb

natives. As always, Nansen was infinitely concerned with everything that went on about him. He studied the natives, their language and customs. He observed the geology of the surrounding region, the birds, the animals, and even the fish in the sea. He learned to handle a kayak and was quick to realize the unique advantages of this versatile craft.

On April 15, 1889, the steamer *Hvidbjornen* arrived to take them home. They said good-bye to their Greenland friends, and on May 21 landed in Copenhagen. As Nansen and his small party came down the gangway, thousands of people lined the pier, cheering, shouting, applauding. The story of their success had preceded them via Nansen's letter to Gamel, and now it seemed that half of Scandinavia was here to welcome them home.

Wherever they turned, crowds of reporters gathered around them, blocking their way, asking questions, pestering them for interviews. For a man of Nansen's modest temperament, this persistent attention soon became annoying.

"Are you glad to be back, Dr. Nansen?"

"Extremely. It was a wonderful experience, but we're all glad to be home."

"Is it true you found a race of gigantic men called snow giants living on top of the glaciers?"

Nansen grinned amiably. "No, there is absolutely no life of any consequence on the ice cap. With the exception of a tiny snow bunting we saw nothing."

"Tell us about the time you were lost."

"We were never lost. We always knew exactly where we were and where we were going."

"There's talk going around that two of your men were frozen to death and that you left them behind buried in a crevasse. Would you care to comment on that?"

Nansen was becoming irritated. "We all came back safe and sound," he said sharply. He waved a hand toward Sverdrup, Balto and the others. "Count us," he said. "See for yourself."

"But what about the time you were starving? Did the possibility of cannibalism ever enter your mind?"

Nansen spun around, fury flashing in his eyes. "Now look here, all this is nothing but wild speculation. There never was any starving, we saw no giants and we were never lost. If you must have a lot of sensational lies to fill up your newspapers, you'll have to find them somewhere else."

"You mean to tell us there wasn't even a mutiny?"

With a shrug of disgust, Nansen turned on his heel, shouldering his way through the crowd, leaving the astounded reporters grumbling at the pier.

That evening, there were parades and festivities for the returning celebrities. Dinners were given, speeches made and medals presented until far into the night.

But if Copenhagen provided a welcome, Nansen's home town of Christiania offered a hero's return. Dozens of ships met his small boat, escorting it in with pennants waving, whistles blowing and streamers flying, while thousands of Norwegians lined the pier, shouting themselves hoarse. Twelve months ago Nansen had set out on a fool's errand; today he returned a conquering hero.

At that time, Norway was a vassal of Sweden, partially governed and controlled by what Norwegians considered a foreign power. Yet they still remembered their own days of greatness, the days of Leif Ericson, King Magnus, Olaf the chieftain, and Eric the Red; and as the years passed, they had yearned for a new hero. Now, here he was, a tall, blond, modern-day Viking, daring and bold, in the person of Fridtjof Nansen. They took him to their hearts, and he became their symbol and their hope. They had no inkling of the great achievements ahead; what he had just accomplished was enough.

For weeks, Nansen was the toast of Norway at parties and gatherings, lionized and fawned over. Unused to pretense and show, he began shying away from the crowds and, after the first hectic weeks of homecoming, took to the woods and ski trails in search of solitude and peace of mind.

One afternoon he was skiing down Frogner Saeter, a ski slope just outside of Christiania, and came upon an attractive young lady half-buried in the snow, struggling to get to her feet. Quickly, he reached down to give her a helping hand.

She accepted it grudgingly, then stood brushing herself off.

Nansen smiled and tried desperately to think of something to say. Finally he stammered, "My name is Fridtjof Nansen."

The girl looked him straight in the eye, without pretext or embarrassment. "Yes," she said. "Everybody knows you."

"Thank you," said Nansen. "I've a strange feeling we've met before."

"I am Professor Sars's daughter," she explained.

"Why, of course, Eva Sars, the singer. Everyone around here knows you, too."

She smiled coyly. "Everyone except you."

"You mustn't include me," he said. "I've been away."

"I know — to Italy and Greenland and before that to the Arctic."

They started walking down the trail, Nansen shouldering the skis. "Suppose we stop at the village for coffee. You can tell me all about yourself, because apparently I've got a lot of catching up to do."

They sat around the small table at the inn, listening to the cedar logs crackling in the fireplace, and she told him all about her interest in books and skiing and about her music and the hopeful career that lay ahead. They talked until the early twilight began casting its soft shadows through the frosted windows.

They walked home together, happy in their newfound companionship, and in a few days it was almost as if they had known each other all their lives. They discussed books and science and art and took long ski hikes into the mountains. Eva was intelligent and understanding, and as the weeks passed, Nansen told her of his hopes, his dreams and his ambitions. She listened intently, since this young, blond giant had come to be her life and her very reason for existence.

One night a few weeks later, Nansen went to the home of his stepsister on the outskirts of Christiania. It was late, and the house was in darkness. Undaunted, he picked up a handful of pebbles and threw them at the bedroom window. A light went on, and a sleepy head appeared. It was his brother-in-law. "Who is there?"

"I, Fridtjof. I want to come in."

"The devil you say. It's two o'clock in the morning. Are you crazy?"

"Yes, completely, and I want to tell you about it."

A moment later, Nansen was in the living room, his sister and brother-in-law standing there in their nightshirts. "What in heaven's name is the matter?" his sister asked.

"I'm going to be married."

"You're joking?"

Nansen was grinning from ear to ear. "I've never been more serious in my life."

"To whom?"

"To Eva Sars, of course."

His sister gasped. "Does the poor girl know what she's letting herself in for?"

"Yes, I've already told her."

"But what about her career, her singing?"

"She's going to give up all that," said Nansen.

His brother-in-law shook his head in amazement. "Well, how you're going to raise a family and go gadding off exploring the North Pole all at the same time is more than I can understand."

They all laughed, and in spite of the late hour Nansen's sister got out cold roast beef and his brother-in-law went down into the cellar for a bottle of wine. This called for a celebration.

Some weeks later, when Sverdrup heard the news, he wrote, "I've lain awake the whole night thinking about it. It's wonderful, of course, and the deuce only knows why I'm so glad, for I suppose it's all up with our North Pole trip now."

Nansen wrote back, "The polar expedition is still on. I told Eve about it the night I proposed, and she agreed that we should go through with it."

The Wheel of Ice

EVA SARS HAD AGREED, but within her heart there were secret and hidden reservations. She had been a spoiled child, raised by doting and indulgent parents, and she could be fiercely independent. Now, she submerged herself completely in her new life as the wife of a famous explorer, learning to understand his purpose, gaining faith in his dreams, hope in his ambitions.

Yet, like most women, she longed for a quiet family life, secure and untroubled, away from the heady uproar of fame and free from the nagging fear that her husband might be lost or killed. She was to have little enough contentment during her short life.

She and Nansen were married in the fall of 1889, and for a honeymoon Nansen took her on a lecture tour of Europe and then on to England, where they attended the International Geographical Congress. Here she listened to long-winded debates on the structure of the earth and the evolution of mountains. They spent six carefree days in Paris, and then went home in time for Nansen to receive the coveted Vega medal, an award given by the Swedish Anthropological and Geographical Society. The medal was presented to Nansen by King Oscar of Sweden.

With each award, Nansen felt a deep sense of guilt. He argued rightly that every member of the expedition had risked his life and endured the burden of hardships the same way as he did, and was equally entitled to the rewards. So when the awards were conferred, he received them humbly and gratefully in the name of the entire crew.

Christiania was a growing town now and to get away from the hustle of the city, Nansen arranged to have a home built at Svartebukta on the shores of Black Bay, where he had hunted ducks as a boy. The house was to be built by Eva's cousin, the architect, Hjalmar Welhaven.

While it was under construction, Nansen and Eva lived in a pavilion near the Lysaker railway station. It was a cold, damp building with a leaky roof and cracked walls through which the winter winds blew incessantly. Nansen was used to roughing it, but Eva found it almost unbearable. She called it the dog hutch and years later would remember how the water froze in the pitchers overnight.

It was here that Nansen started his book on Greenland. He wrote page after page in a sweeping handwriting, compiling from his notes and diary. He worked diligently from early morning till late at night, seldom taking time for rest or relaxation. When he did, it was always to talk with Eva, telling her of his plans and hopes. She faced the first realization of what lay ahead as she learned the full details of his proposed expedition to the Pole.

He drew maps for her on pieces of scrap paper, showing her Mohn's theory of how the Arctic current sweeps across the North Pole, moving the ice with it like a gigantic wheel.

She watched him as he spoke, his blue-grey eyes animated and alive, his handsome face set in grim determination, and she knew he would have to do this thing above everything else. "You want to be the first man to the Pole?" she asked.

"No, that is only of secondary importance," said Nansen. "First I want to test Mohn's theory, to prove that the Arctic is a vast shallow sea of ice turning slowly about the polar axis of the earth. If I can do this, it will be of great importance to oceanography and a tremendous boon to the science of weather forecasting."

"Then you admit it's only a theory?"

Nansen agreed. "Yes, but we have a lot of evidence to back it up, and I believe Mohn is right. With the proper backing and the right equipment, we can prove it once and for all."

Eva was silent for a moment; then she spoke. "This means a great deal to you?"

"It means everything."

"Would you give it up if I asked?"

"Only if *you* asked."

"How long will you be gone?"

"Three, maybe four years. I don't know."

"And during all this time I will have no word. I will not know where you are, how you are or even if you are alive."

Nansen sighed, staring out the window at the gently falling snow. "No, I'm afraid not."

She got up, turning her back and biting her lip to hold back the tears. "Let's go over and look at the house," she said, putting on her coat. "Hjalmar tells me it will be finished by March."

They moved in at the end of the winter, long before the house was ready. It was a huge, rambling structure, situated on a secluded inlet. In front was a thinly wooded slope leading down to the bay where the fjord ran out to sea. They called it "Godthaab," meaning Good Hope. The rooms were large and spacious, the walls of heavy unfinished timber, the rafters and beams rough and unpainted. It was completely rustic, with carved pine furniture and chairs upholstered in primitive Nordic designs. To add a contrasting note of elegance, Eva's enormous grand piano stood in the middle of the drawing room.

In Nansen's study were his books and trophies, guns, polar bear rugs and walrus hides, with a large portrait of Eva dominating the room.

In this house, their first child was born, a baby girl with a round cherubic face, resembling her mother but with her father's blondness and grey-blue eyes. They called her Liv, meaning life, and felt that she made the little household complete.

During the next few years, Nansen grew busier. He had finished his book on Greenland, a massive volume of 800 pages including the history, geology and anthropology of this vast island, along with a day-by-day description of the exciting race across the ice. He was curator of the University Museum at Christiania and hard at work on his new book about the Eskimo.

Yet his thoughts were never far from his forthcoming

Nansen as a young man, with portrait of Eva and little Liv in the background

polar expedition, and he began planning for it. He took Eva on long ski trips into the mountains, testing sleeping bags and ski harnesses. She plodded behind him mile after mile, cold, tired and often hungry.

She adored this big, overgrown, boyish Viking and would have followed him anywhere. She posed for him when he needed a model for his Eskimo sketches, she listened patiently as he read pages of his manuscript and she sang to him when he was tired and needed diversion. On the mountain trail, in the dead of winter, she even helped him test his new concoctions of pemmican. Eva stood freezing in the snow while he fed her spoonfuls of the greasy stuff, her eyes closed, her pretty face contorted with disgust.

"Swallow it," he said. "It's good for you. It'll keep you warm and give you energy."

An hour later, after they had trudged another three miles, he asked, "How do you feel now?"

"Fine," she lied. "Just fine." She was half-starved, but she didn't dare admit it.

"More pemmican?"

She shook her head vigorously. "No, I've had enough, thank you." Then she watched as he shovelled whole spoonfuls of the stuff into his mouth, licking his lips as though it were some kind of candy. Her stomach revolted, and she had to turn away and remark how beautiful the sky looked with the sun setting behind the distant mountains.

And all the while the day she dreaded was drawing ever closer, the day when he would go off into the far unknown, for months, for years, maybe forever.

The great hall of the Royal Geographical Society was crowded, filled to overflowing with members and guests.

THE WHEEL OF ICE

Even the balconies and aisles were jammed. To Nansen, it seemed as if all of London were there.

Standing on the speaker's platform, he looked out across the sea of faces and felt his heart pounding in his chest. Seated in the audience were some of the most famous explorers in the world. They were knighted conquerors of the earth, bearded, white-haired pioneers of the Arctic, grizzled old mariners and prominent men of science. Most of them had gained immortality and fame long before he was born, others while he was still a schoolboy. As a youngster, he had followed their adventures avidly, secretly hoping to follow in their footsteps. Now, in 1892, he stood before them in the spacious hall of the Royal Geographical Society, to tell them of his plans, to ask their help, to seek their advice.

There was Admiral Sir George Nares, commander of the famous ship *Challenger,* which sailed on the first round-the-world oceanographic expedition, and master of the renowned HMS *Discovery.* Next to him sat Admiral Sir Francis Leopold McClintock, explorer extraordinary and discoverer of the ill-fated Sir John Franklin's expedition. Here, too, was Commodore Sir Albert Markham, the man who had penetrated farther north than any other man in history. And behind them were rows of other distinguished adventurers: Admiral Sir Edward Inglefield, Admiral Sir Erasmus Ommanney, Dr. John Rae, Captain Joseph Wiggins, Sir Allen Young, Captain Wharton, Director of the Hydrographic Department of England, and scores of others.

Nansen recognized them all, the greats and the near-greats. He looked down at them now, glancing from face to face, wondering if they had come here to mark him as a brash young intruder or to listen sincerely to what he had to say. He would soon find out.

He began his talk with a brief summary of polar exploration, then went on to outline his daring plan.

"I firmly believe that the only practical route into the heart of the Arctic is by following the drift of the polar current. That such a current exists is plainly demonstrated by a number of sources, of which the well-known *Jeannette* expedition is a prime example. While exploring an open lead off the Siberian mainland, the sailing ship *Jeannette* became frozen fast in the ice in the vicinity of Wrangel Island. She finally sank, in 1879, off the New Siberia Islands, and three years later some articles of clothing and a few pages of her supply records were found floating on the ice at the southern tip of Greenland, 3,000 miles away.

"Professor Henrick Mohn examined these articles and positively identified them as belonging to the *Jeannette*. He further concluded that they must have reached Greenland by means of an extensive current flowing in a clockwise direction across the face of the Arctic."

Nansen looked up, waiting for the import of his statement to take effect. "In other words, gentlemen, had the *Jeannette* been able to withstand the pressures of the ice, she, too, might have drifted safely across the Arctic and along the way might well have moved close to the polar axis of the earth."

There was a low murmur of conversation as the distinguished members commented on this new and unheard-of theory.

"If further proof is necessary," Nansen continued, "there is additional evidence in the great masses of driftwood constantly found along the eastern shores of Greenland. The German polar expedition collected specimens of this wood and found it to be composed largely of fir, larch and alder, all species commonly native to the Siberian mainland.

"In still another instance, samples of sediment lodged between the crevasses of the drift ice off the coast of Greenland were analyzed by Professor Cleve of Upsala. These were found to contain species of diatoms native only to the Bering Strait. In every case, these foreign objects were discovered over 3,000 miles from their point of origin and could have reached their final destination in only one way. That is by means of a major ocean current flowing across the top of the world, in an erratic but persistent clockwise direction.

"To me this evidence is conclusive. I firmly believe there is such a current and that it can be put to use to advance our knowledge of this important area of the globe.

"I intend to build a ship, a small but sturdy vessel able to withstand the pressures of the ice, a ship designed to rise above the floe instead of being crushed by it. In such a vessel, a team of scientists will be able to drift leisurely across the Arctic, perhaps even over the Pole itself, making important investigations in the fields of oceanography, meteorology, astronomy, physics and zoology. They would live and work as comfortably and safely as they would in a laboratory here at home."

He closed his notes on the lectern and glanced up, trying to assess the audience reaction. "Gentlemen, this, then, is my plan. With forethought, careful preparation and the right equipment, I have every reason to believe it will be successful. As experienced travellers who have travelled far in the regions I intend to sail, I trust you will share my optimism. Thank you for your attention."

Slowly, a hubbub of conversation spread through the hall, then diminished as old Admiral Sir Francis Leopold McClintock got to his feet. Resplendent in his dark blue uniform with its epaulets and gold braid, he held up his hand for silence, speaking in a deep, resonant voice full of authority. "This is truly an adventurous plan. Dr. Nansen is to be commended for his bravery and enthusiasm. However, I doubt that bravery alone will be sufficient proof against the tremendous power of the Arctic ice. It might be possible to construct a ship able to withstand the buffeting of the loose summer ice floe, but the violent pressures of the winter pack ice are an entirely different matter. Any ship caught in the grip of such enormous forces must inevitably be doomed. She would never be heard from again. Under the circumstances, I cannot bring myself to sanction this daring scheme. It goes much too far beyond any hope of success."

McClintock had barely finished when Admiral Nares jumped to his feet. "I am in full accord with Admiral McClintock's views. As a man of the sea, I can only repeat the well-known axiom of Arctic navigation, and that is to stay well clear of the ice. Dr. Nansen proposes to do just the opposite and sail his craft directly into the ice pack in an effort to become locked within its crushing jaws. This is a most foolhardy project and one that is destined to meet with certain disaster.

"I also disagree with Dr. Nansen on the existence of an Arctic current. From firsthand observation, I can unequivocally state that the ice floe is moved about in a haphazard fashion by the vagaries of the prevailing winds. To place oneself and one's ship at the mercy of these unpredictable elements would be highly imprudent, to say the least. If Dr. Nansen would be content to limit his operations to such tasks as could easily be performed along the edge of the ice fields, I believe his efforts would be of greater benefit to the advancement of science."

Next, the elderly traveller, Sir Allen Young, got up to speak. "It is extremely likely that Dr. Nansen will find a

THE WHEEL OF ICE

considerable land mass blocking his way across the Arctic. This precludes the possibility of a current and makes folly of any plan to drift across the Pole. Dr. Nansen would be wise to consider this carefully before sailing into a trap from which he may not be able to extricate himself."

Now, the great hall was buzzing with excitement, while the secretary of the society tried to make himself heard above the commotion in order to read a letter from the venerable Sir Joseph Dalton Hooker, the botanist. "There are many dangers involved in a voyage such as Dr. Nansen proposes, not the least of which is scurvy. On an expedition of such long duration, where the supply of fresh fruits and vegetables must of necessity be limited, the risk in health and life would be most serious. Let us hope that Dr. Nansen will modify his plans and use his skill and courage in a less perilous attempt to solve the mysteries of the Arctic."

For the next two hours, the protests and criticism continued, punctuated by a few small voices of encouragement. At the end of this time, Nansen arose to make his final comment.

"I wish to thank you for your advice and counsel. They are well taken and I know you have only my safety and the safety of my crew at heart. Unfortunately, no area of exploration, no pioneering into the unknown has ever been without its share of danger, without its element of risk. This has always been so. There is no safe path into the future, for that path has not yet been charted.

"So in spite of your well-meant warnings and admonitions, I stand firm in my resolution. Included in my plans will be every precaution for the health and safety of my crew. Then, as we did in Greenland, we will burn our bridges behind us. The only direction will be forward."

Now, notwithstanding their early misgivings, the society rose as one man in a wild round of applause. They might frown on recklessness and pretension, but they admired humility and courage.

Old Admiral McClintock made himself heard. "Dr. Nansen speaks with the bold tongue of a Viking. His plan is more romantic than scientific, for only a daring and creative mind could have conceived such a scheme. With him go our hopes and our prayers. We wish him Godspeed and a safe return, and we will all breathe easier when he is back once again within our midst."

This time, Nansen did not have to beg for support. His own country came to his aid, voting him two-thirds of the total sum, with the understanding that the expedition should be an entirely Norwegian venture. The remaining third was raised through private sources and, not to be remiss, even the Royal Geographical Society offered a grant of 300 pounds sterling.

Now the plans could go forward. Equipment and provisions could be ordered and tested; the men could be selected. But first there was the all-important matter of the ship. Nansen knew she must be strong and sturdy, not too large nor too small, with just the proper curve to allow her to slip out of the ice, yet with enough stability to ride out the Arctic storms. On her depended the lives of the men, the very success of the expedition. The ship was to be their passport to victory.

North with the Fram

IN THE JOINER'S SHOP at the shipyard on Rekevik Bay, a seaport in Iceland, Nansen and a famous Norwegian shipbuilder, Colin Archer, inspected the small wooden model of the three-masted schooner. Colin Archer, with his long, white beard, his bushy hair and bristling eyebrows, resembled a character out of a Bible story. His strong, gnarled hands bespoke the craftsman, the builder of ships. He was known up and down Scandinavia for his genius in nautical design. His pilot ships and lifeboats were the best in Europe.

With a steady forefinger, he drew an imaginary line down across the bow. "By increasing the angle blocks, we can arch the stem for more slope," he said in a thick Scottish accent. "The one disadvantage is she'll be apt to roll a good deal more in heavy seas."

"I've thought of that," said Nansen. "But it can't be

Colin Archer

helped. If the curve of the hull will help resist the direct pressure of the ice, then that's what we've got to have."

"All right," said the shipbuilder. "I'll draw up a new design and make another model. It should be ready within a few weeks."

Nansen walked to the door, inhaling the pungent smell of new cut pine, his feet shuffling through piles of wood shavings on the floor. He stopped with his hand on the knob. "You are a patient man, Mr. Archer. This is the eighth modification I've asked for, and we haven't even started yet."

Colin Archer smiled. "You forget I'm in this as much as you are. My reputation is at stake, too."

"But the theory is mine," said Nansen. "If she goes down, only I am to blame."

The older man tugged thoughtfully at his beard. "She won't go down, Dr. Nansen. I vouch for that. She'll be the strongest ship ever built."

After months of trial and error a working design was agreed upon. The keel was laid, and slowly the gaunt skeleton of the 400-ton vessel rose on its cradle. The frames were lifted into position and bolted fast, each joint reinforced with heavy bands of steel. All stanchions, knees, braces and footings were constructed of sturdy Italian oak for durability and firmness. Her planking was composed of three layers, with an outer section of tough, solid greenheart making an impenetrable bulkhead 24 to 28 inches thick. The ship was 128 feet long overall, pointed fore and aft, without external projections of any kind. Constructed as an ordinary three-masted schooner, her rigging was simple and functional. She was the first vessel ever built for the express purpose of coping with the powerful forces of the Arctic ice.

On October 26, 1892, Nansen climbed the tall scaffolding constructed around the front of the ship. With Eva and a small group of dignitaries, he looked out over the tiny inlet where hundreds of spectators gathered along the rocky shoreline to witness the christening. There was a brief ceremony on the platform, then Eva lifted a bottle of champagne and smashed it against the curving bow. "Fram *skal den hede*," she said, meaning in English, "She shall be called *Fram*, or *Forward*."

The little red pennant was run up on its staff, the last moorings were cut away and the vessel slid down the ways and into the water. Colin Archer closed his eyes and mumbled a silent prayer as she bobbed on the surface, sending a succession of bow waves splashing against the distant shore.

As the months passed, her deck gear and rigging were completed, and heavily laden vans rolled down to the dock delivering a steady stream of supplies and equipment. There were cases of scientific instruments, microscopes, thermometers, theodolites, sextants, electroscopes,

DESIGNS FOR THE "FRAM"

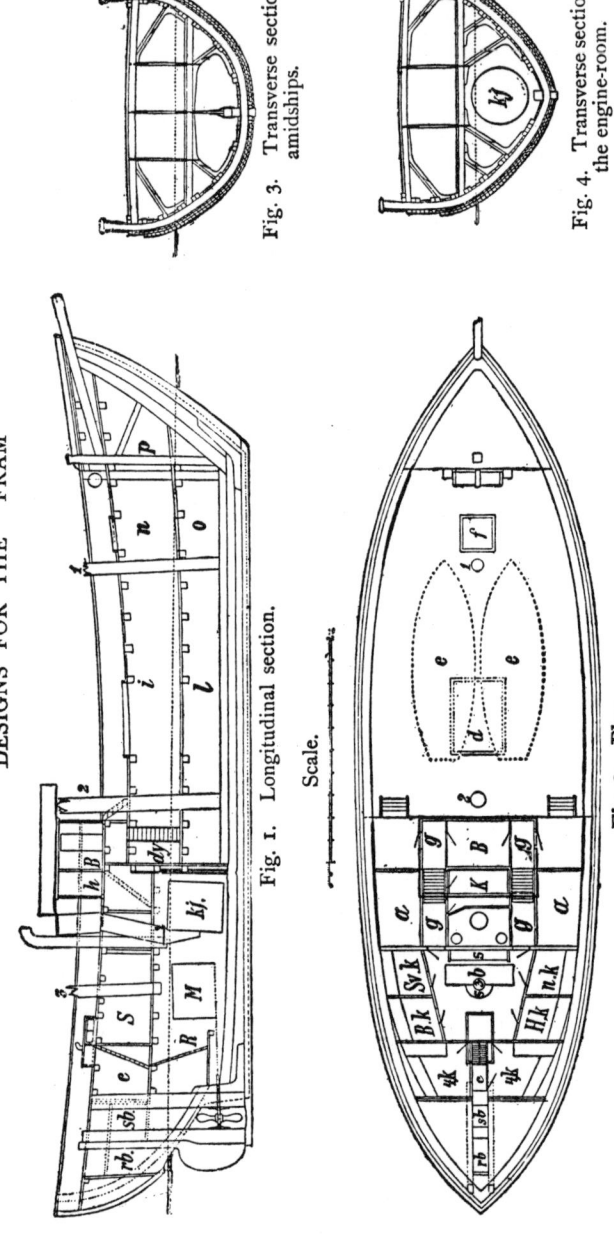

Fig. 1. Longitudinal section.

Fig. 2. Plan.

Fig. 3. Transverse section amidships.

Fig. 4. Transverse section at the engine-room.

rb Rudder-well. *sb* Propeller-well. *S* Saloon. *s* Sofas in saloon. *b* Table in saloon. *Svk* Sverdrup's cabin. *Bk* Blessing's cabin. *4k* Four-berth cabins. *Hk* Scott-Hansen's cabin. *nk* Nansen's cabin. *c* Way down to engine-room. *R* Engine-room. *M* Engine. *kj* Boiler. *K* Cook's galley. *B* Chart-room. *h* Work-room. *dy* Place for the dynamo. *d* Main-hatch. *g* Companions leading from saloon. *l* Under-hold. *f* Fore-hatch. *n* Fore-hold. *o* Under fore-hold. *p* Pawl-Lit. *e* Long boats. *i* Main-hold. *1* Foremast. *2* Mainmast. *3* Mizzenmast.

water samplers and magnetic measuring devices. Coils of rope, sounding line, fishnets, trawls and plankton traps were stored below decks.

From all over the world came crates of foodstuffs and provisions: pork, corned beef and bacon from Europe; dried fish, lime juice and coffee from England; jams and cranberry sauce from America; 1,300 pounds of the best Danish butter, plus canned vegetables, pemmican, chocolate, sugar and hundreds of boxes of dog biscuits.

Carloads of textbooks, reference volumes and journals were hauled aboard, enough to fill a small library, while an entire collection of rifles, revolvers, harpoons and signal cannon were stacked in the arms room. To care for the health and welfare of the crew, there were medicine chests stocked with pills, ointments, bandages, compresses, splints and surgical instruments.

Every item, every tool or implement that could possibly be of any use was brought along. The little expedition would have to be completely self-sufficient.

Then, on a gloomy midsummer day in June, 1893, the *Fram* was ready to sail. The sky was dark and overcast, and a heavy grey mist hung in the air. At "Godthaab" Nansen wrote his final letters. When he had finished, he closed the door of his study for the last time and went down the steps to the veranda where Eva waited with the baby. He kissed his wife affectionately and took little Liv in his arms.

The child brushed a soft, tiny hand across his face, giggling happily. Nansen looked down at her, holding her close, his eyes filling with tears. "You laugh, little one," he said. "But I — " He was unable to finish the sentence. Quickly, he gave the child back to her mother and, turning abruptly, walked down the path to the waiting launch. He stood in the bow as the small boat sped across the water, feeling the sting of the salt spray blowing against his face.

Here was the culmination of his long years of planning. His hopes and his dreams had finally come true. By right, he should be filled with a warm feeling of pride and elation. Instead, he experienced a deep sense of sadness and a strange, melancholy depression.

When he reached the *Fram,* Nansen climbed the ladder to the deck, greeting no one and going straight to the bridge. The headlands of Norway were stretching out to sea, and with one quick, backward glance he saw the hazy outline of "Godthaab" and a young woman standing on the shore, a child in her arms.

His voice was cracked and unsteady as he spoke to the man at the helm. "You may weigh anchor, Mr. Hansen," he said, "whenever you are ready."

When news of the expedition had first been announced, letters came pouring in from Europe and America, from as far away as Australia. Adventure-loving men, young and old, from all over the world wanted to go along. But Nansen, bound by his original promise, selected a crew from among his own countrymen.

Together with Otto Sverdrup, who was to be captain and master of the little vessel, there were thirteen in all. Some of them were experienced explorers, many had sailed the Arctic seas as whalers, fishermen or seal hunters. They were young, strong men, full of spirit and adventure, and there was much good-natured banter and horseplay. They were all in top physical condition, capable of great endurance in the most difficult situations. Hjalmar Johansen, the young stoker, set the standard for all when he demonstrated his fitness by walking on his hands across the length of the main deck, then down the forward ladder and into the cabin.

Escorted by fleets of steamers, sailing craft and small boats, the *Fram* sailed down the fjord and out to the Skagerrak. Hundreds of people lined the way, cheering, shouting, waving good-bye. As she swung clear, around the tip of Norway, her compass needle pointed north northeast. For the first few days, the weather was bad, and the little ship rolled like a barrel, her decks and scuppers awash, the water swirling around the longboats, the stacks of timber and barrels stored on deck.

For twenty-six days they hugged the coastline, stopping at Bergen and Tromsö, on the west coast of Norway, and Vardo, well up within the Arctic Circle. On the twentieth of July, they waved their final good-bye to Norway. At Khabarova, high on the northern coast of Russia, they stopped to pick up the sled dogs: tough, wiry Siberian huskies.

A few days later, they encountered their first ice fields and felt their way cautiously into the Kara Sea. To augment their supply of fresh meat, they made short excursions across the surrounding tundra in search of wild ducks, reindeer and bear.

Early one morning, Nansen was awakened by Peter Henriksen, the expedition's harpooner. "Quick," said Henriksen. "There's a big herd of walrus lying on the pack ice just off the port bow."

Nansen jumped out of his bunk, pulling on his clothes. He stopped in the chart room for a rifle and cartridges; then, together with Henriksen and the cook, Adolf Juell, he climbed into a small boat and headed for the sleeping animals.

It was a beautifully clear morning, extremely cold with an azure-blue sky overhead, and they could plainly see the great beasts crowded together on an ice floe some distance away. They were enormous animals, tawny

The "Fram" leaving Bergen, July 1893

brown with thick, loose-fitting hides, wrinkled and furrowed. Sharp ivory tusks protruded 15 inches from under fat, bewhiskered snouts.

In the middle of the sleeping herd a huge bull lifted his head from time to time, sniffing the air, searching for danger.

The small boat glided along silently, Juell at the oars, Henriksen in the bow, harpoon ready for the throw. Nansen stood behind him with the rifle. Slowly, they crept ahead, the dipping oars barely rippling the bright green water while the great white expanse of ice stretched about them into the far horizon. Everything was still save for the gentle lapping of the waves against the boat.

Juell lifted the oars to balance the small craft as Henriksen shifted position.

"Easy," whispered Nansen. "Not too soon. We've got to get closer."

The unsuspecting herd lay quiet with only an occasional grunt or a languid wave of a huge flipper.

Nansen held his breath, his rifle poised, as slowly they inched closer and closer, the long seconds ticking by like an eternity. Then suddenly the silence was broken by a sharp grating sound as the bow scraped along the submerged edge of the ice floe. Instantly, every head came up, looming into the air, towering over the puny men, dark, beady eyes glowering, muzzles bristling with anger.

Nansen waited the barest fraction of a second, then shouted, "Now!"

With a mighty heave, Henriksen threw the deadly weapon straight toward the big bull. It sped through the air, flashing in the bright sunlight, struck the beast a glancing blow high on the shoulder and bounced harmlessly off, clattering to the ice.

A walrus hunt (from a painting by Otto Sinding)

In a wild surge of panic, the entire herd turned, snorting and bellowing with rage, charging for the little boat. Desperately, Juell strained at the oars in an effort to get clear. Blinded by the spray, Nansen fired point-blank into the lumbering mass of creatures as they hit the water barely inches away from the boat. The sea became a boiling eddy of foam and froth as the enraged animals floundered in the bloodstained water, pitching the small craft about like a chip of wood. At any moment, Nansen expected to be thrown into the water and cut to ribbons by the murderous tusks.

All around them, huge heads bobbed to the surface, bellowing with rage, roaring defiance. Drenched with spray, Nansen searched the frenzied herd for the two he had wounded. He spotted them a moment later in the melee. Risking a chance of being capsized, he had Juell approach the crippled beasts and finish them off, each with a shot through the head. They struggled for a moment, then turned belly up in the crimson water. The remainder of the herd dispersed, and with frozen fingers Nansen and Henriksen reached down and secured the two dead animals, tying ropes around their tusks.

When they were dragged up on the ice, Adolf Juell got his first good look at a full-grown walrus. Fully ten feet long, they were as fat and round as young whales. "Good grief!" he exclaimed. "What a lot of meat!"

The entire herd had disappeared by now, and the *Fram* moved in to haul the huge carcasses up on deck, where they were cut into sections and stored in the ice locker.

Having replenished the meat supply, they continued on, sailing north northwest, skirting the edge of the ice field all the way, each day creeping closer to their destination.

By September 19, they had reached 76 degrees latitude, a great deal farther north than they had expected to penetrate. Drift ice was visible on either side, but there was open water ahead.

Nansen looked up to the crow's nest where Henriksen was standing watch. He saw the big man lean down, his

A sleepy walrus (pastel sketch by Nansen)

hands cupped around his mouth, and over the sound of the wind he heard the words, "All clear, all clear."

Nansen shook his head. It was almost too good to be true. Later, he spoke to Sverdrup about it. "Seventy-seven degrees and still no sign of the pack ice."

"Aye," said Sverdrup. "And we'll do even better. I wager we'll reach 84 or maybe 85 degrees before we freeze in." They were silent for a moment, then Sverdrup continued. "We might even sail straight on to the Pole. It could be open water, you know."

Nansen smiled at Sverdrup's easy optimism. "Not likely, or it would have been discovered before this," he said.

Yet, in spite of his doubts, they continued to sail on, mile after mile. A few days later, he was in the chart room, plotting their course, reflecting on their good luck, when suddenly he felt the ship vibrate as its engines were thrown into reverse. He rushed up on deck and looked out over the bow. There, directly in front of the *Fram,* was a solid wall of ice like a great ragged mantle of white, and Nansen knew they had reached the outer ramparts of the Arctic ice pack. Now, they would sail no more but would freeze in, like a stone in concrete, and hopefully drift across the top of the world.

With pinions and hawsers, the *Fram* was made fast to the nearest floe. For three long years, this desolate wasteland of ice and snow was to be their home and their refuge.

Nansen glanced up at the heavy grey sky and saw small flocks of snipe and plover winging their way south. He knew that the long polar night was not far away.

Now, the big rudder was hauled up out of its well, the engine was dismantled, each part carefully oiled and stored away. Workshops were set up for the car-

Reading temperatures with lens

penters, electricians and smithy, and a large windmill erected on the foredeck to provide electricity for light and power.

Little by little, the ice closed in around the *Fram*, locking her in a relentless grip. The days became increasingly short and the crew settled down to a steady routine of work and activity.

Young Scott-Hansen, the expedition's meteorologist, measured wind velocities, recorded temperatures and studied the movements of the celestial bodies while Theodore Jacobsen, the mate of the *Fram*, and Ivar Mogstad, the carpenter, lowered heavy weights through holes in the ice to measure the depth of the Arctic Sea.

All work began at eight o'clock in the morning. Lars Pettersen, the blacksmith, sharpened knives, forged hardware and soldered utensils. Anton Amundsen repaired instruments and watches and kept the ship's machinery in working order, while the sailmaker, Bernt Bentzen, manufactured dog harnesses, canvas boots and leather products. Bernhard Nordahl, the electrician, tended the batteries and dynamos and saw to it that the lighting system continued to function properly.

Adolf Juell served meals equal to anything found in the best restaurants of Europe. His menus included soups, chowder, beef, pork, roasts, stews, venison, potatoes, green vegetables, puddings, cakes and pastries, coffee, tea and hot chocolate.

The workday ended with the evening meal, after which the men read, played cards or listened to the music of the organ. Dr. Henrik Blessing, the ship's physician, published a weekly newspaper, a small one-page missive called "Framsjaa." With each man performing his assigned task, the little ship soon became a warm, comfortable home.

By October 9 the *Fram* was completely frozen in, as great masses of ice piled up around her bow, and now the grinding pressures of the winter ice began their slow, relentless advance. The men were down in the saloon just finishing the midday meal when suddenly a series of rumbling explosions shook the little vessel. Instinctively, Nansen put down his fork, his hands gripping the edge of the table. It had taken him by surprise, but he recognized it for what it was, the first crushing pressures of the ice. Day after day, it would go on growing in power and intensity, and the *Fram* would undergo her long-awaited test of strength and endurance.

He looked about the small room, glancing from face to face, trying to estimate the men's reactions. Some of them had stopped eating and sat tense and expectant. Others were staring up at the deck beams, waiting.

For a long moment, there was complete silence, then once again a loud, groaning thunder shook the ice, and the *Fram* was lifted bodily several feet into the air.

Quickly, the men jumped to their feet, hanging onto the bulkhead for support. They looked from one to another, fully aware that their very existence depended on the outcome of this elemental struggle. One by one, they rushed up on deck even as the vessel was shaken by new waves of violence.

From the vantage point of a nearby pressure ridge, Nansen saw the *Fram* heave and buckle then slip higher and higher, inch by inch surmounting the persistent pressure, exactly as she had been designed to do. All afternoon, the heavy vibrations continued, coming in wave upon wave, and each time the little ship lurched and groaned, shifting position like a living thing fighting for its life. And all the while, Nansen paced back and forth watching the battle, silently mumbling a prayer of thanks to a bearded old man named Colin Archer.

10

The Long Drift

BY THE MIDDLE OF OCTOBER, the activity on board the *Fram* had settled down to a steady, easygoing pace. Occasionally, the little ship was snowed in by violent storms that kept the men below decks for days at a time. Now and then, a prowling polar bear was seen nosing about the vicinity, attracted by the huge, alien object with its tempting smells. Except for such minor incidents, life went along serene and unhurried.

One crisp, cold morning, Nansen decided to change the routine by trying his hand at driving the dogs. He hitched up six of the best animals, harnessing them securely to the sled. Then, with his usual aplomb, he climbed aboard and gave the command to start.

The dogs had been cooped up for months and were restless and eager to go. They took off, flying, racing across the ice at a terrific speed Round and round they went, circling the ship in a wide arc. For a few minutes, Fridtjof enjoyed the exhilarating ride, giving the dogs a free rein, allowing them to run where they would. But then when he tried to stop them, he was surprised to find that they were completely out of control. He pulled, he yanked and he shouted, but his efforts seemed only to increase their excitement, and they dashed along all the faster. Desperately, he clung to the sled, the wind whistling past his ears, the flying snow stinging his face as the runaway team rattled and bounced over the rough ice. If he tried to guide them to the left, they promptly went off to the right; if he tried to turn them to the right, they stubbornly veered to the left. It was a wild, hectic ride, the frisky animals yapping with delight.

As they made the sharp turn around the bow of the ship, Nansen jumped to the ice and dug in his heels in an attempt to hold back the sled. But the dogs were not easily overruled. They lunged forward with renewed energy, sweeping him off his feet, dragging him along like a bouncing sack of potatoes. Helpless and frustrated, he bellowed with rage, threatening to shoot the lot of them if they didn't stop. It was all to no avail, and the mad, crazy whirl continued until the animals were sufficiently played out to stop of their own accord.

Slowly, Nansen pulled himself to his feet. He walked up and down the line, glowering with anger, berating the animals with every invective he could think of. "Boneheads, featherbrains," he shouted. "You bunch of idiotic malamutes, I could get better cooperation out of a pack of toy poodles."

The panting dogs looked up at him, tails wagging and tongues lolling out of the sides of their mouths.

Ready to try again, Nansen took a firm grip on the sled, braced himself and shouted the command to go.

The whole thing was a repeat performance. The dogs lunged forward with such force that he was immediately pulled off his feet. This time he landed neatly on his backside and was dragged along in a sitting position, leaving a wide furrow in the drifting snow. Bouncing and hurdling over the ruts, he lost his whip, his cap and finally his patience.

After two or three more laps, he managed to bring the team to a halt. Without a word of comment, he unhitched the animals and shoved them back into their kennels, convinced that this was the most undisciplined team of sled dogs that had ever been whelped.

As the days passed, the sun began to sink lower in the heavens, until by the end of October it disappeared completely below the horizon. High amidships, the big windmill whirled and spun, generating light and power for the warm, comfortable cabins below.

Frequently, the relentless pressure of the ice exploded like a great cannonade, shaking the ship from stem to stern, then fading away only to return a few minutes later with even greater force. Occasionally, it reached a roaring crescendo, and the men were forced to shout over the earsplitting din to make themselves heard. Each time, the *Fram* buckled and shook, but she always managed to hold firm, resettling herself into a new position. As time passed, the men gained complete confidence in her ability to endure.

In spite of the subzero temperatures, the dogs were housed in coops up on deck, where they remained healthy and strong. They were used to the snow and the cold, and even in the midst of howling blizzards they simply curled up in their little huts and slept warm and snug. But if they were acclimated to the sudden changes of weather, they were not safe from the ravages of a mysterious nocturnal prowler. Each night, the frightened animals could be heard moving about in their kennels, whimpering with fear. Upon investigation, the watch could find nothing amiss, but each morning when Henriksen or Mogstad went up on deck there was another dog missing.

The mystery remained unsolved until one morning Henriksen came stumbling down the hatch, clutching at his side, the stain of fresh blood seeping through his fingers. "A gun," he shouted. "Give me a gun, quick."

"What's happened?" asked Nansen.

"There's a bear up there," said Henriksen excitedly. "He jumped me as I was making the rounds. Came right out of the darkness, without warning, and nipped me in the side. I bashed him a good one across the nose with the lantern but he's still up there after the dogs."

Without waiting, Nansen reached for his rifle and rushed up on deck followed by Henriksen and Mogstad. There, in the grey darkness, under the stern of the ship, they saw the bear with one of the sled dogs pinned under its great paw. Defiant and bold, it glared up at the men with a savage growl.

Nansen was about to shoot when he realized that he had forgotten to remove the tow plug from the muzzle of his rifle. He spent an anxious minute trying to extract it, while Henriksen stood by frantically clicking the trigger on his own gun as it repeatedly missed fire. In the meantime, the bear was preparing to make a meal of the dog, while Mogstad jumped up and down, shouting and waving his arms in a desperate effort to distract the hungry beast.

Just as the bear reached down to finish off the dog,

Nansen got his rifle clear. With one motion, he brought it to his shoulder and fired. The bear leaped up with an angry snarl, releasing the dog unharmed. Nansen fired again. This time, the bear fell in its tracks. Henriksen, with a superficial wound, was treated by Dr. Blessing.

A short while later, Nansen made a search of the area and found the partly eaten remains of two of the dogs where the hungry bear had left them. In spite of his long experience in the Arctic, Nansen was surprised to find a polar bear prowling so far north in the dead of winter, and he gave strict orders that no one was to venture out on the ice without a rifle.

Like a diminutive wooden toy, the *Fram* lay in the heart of the Arctic drift. Wrapped in the purple gloom of the long polar night, the men had only their timepieces by which to distinguish day and night. Outside of the warm cabins, the temperature continued to drop until it hit the minus forties, remaining there for weeks at a time.

The first Christmas on board was a day of joy and celebration, with a lavish dinner of oxtail soup, roast reindeer, potatoes, peas smothered in melted butter, cloudberries and cream and a wide selection of cakes and pastries. The little saloon was aglow with lights and decorations.

After the meal, two large baskets of gifts were brought out. They had been packed by Scott-Hansen's fiancée, with instructions not to be opened till Christmas. There was something for everyone—a pocketknife for Amundsen, a pipe for Sverdrup, playing cards for Nordahl, cigars for Nansen. Juell, the cook, received a canister of imported Turkish coffee and Johansen a dart game that was immediately set up and put to use. Later in the

THE LONG DRIFT 131

evening, great schooners of bock beer were brought out. The men lit their pipes and gathered around the organ to sing Christmas carols and other holiday melodies. It was a welcome relief from long months of unchanging routine.

A week later, there was another celebration to usher in the new year. Shortly after midnight, Nansen left the party for a quiet, solitary stroll across the ice. It was a beautiful clear night, with the gaudy streamers of the aurora borealis shifting across the heavens. During his walk, he turned and looked back to see the dark masts and rigging of the *Fram* silhouetted against the pale yellow glow of sky. Behind it, the silken draperies of light were shimmering across the heavens like great pulsating rays of violet sheen, intermingled with pastel shades of pink and green. The very air crackled with the brilliant iridescence, lending an eerie glow to the surrounding landscape.

For almost an hour, he stood there, spellbound by this gorgeous display. In the cold silence, he thought of the long months they had already spent in this vast frozen wasteland and the even longer months that might lie ahead. He thought, too, of Norway and of home, and for a fleeting moment he felt an agonizing pang of regret as he conjured up little Liv and Eva waiting for him on the shore. How long would it be before he saw them again? With a shrug of his shoulders, he pushed the thought from his mind and turned his steps back to the *Fram,* to his merry companions and the warm, comfortable cabins.

But life in the Arctic was not all play and celebration; the scientific work went on in spite of darkness and the weather. Young Scott-Hansen and Hjalmar Johansen conducted the meteorological studies, recording temper-

A chronometer observation with the theodolite

atures, magnetic constants, radiation, wind velocities and humidity. Electroscopes were used to determine the amount of electricity in the air, and the frequency and intensity of the aurora borealis were observed and noted. Readings were taken every four hours, day and night, from various locations out on the ice, on deck or high in the crow's nest. In spite of wind and snow, in spite of subzero temperatures, these indomitable men carried on their arduous task.

Careful studies were made on the formation and texture of the surrounding ice pack, and by use of special boring instruments they measured its thickness. In areas away from the accumulated floes, it averaged 8 to 9 feet, but in the immediate vicinity of the *Fram* their longest drills reached down to 30 feet and still could not touch water.

These accurate observations of temperature, winds and ice were the beginnings of polar meteorology, giving the first clear picture of the Arctic air masses and their effect on the entire Northern Hemisphere.

THE LONG DRIFT

At stated intervals, the ship's physician, Dr. Blessing, conducted physical examinations of every member of the crew. Each man was weighed, tested and examined. Blood samples were taken to determine hemoglobin and the number of red corpuscles. Surprisingly enough, even after a year in the frozen North they were all in excellent condition. With good food, regular hours of work and play and plenty of outdoor exercise, they remained in perfect health and actually gained weight during the course of the long voyage.

Astronomical observations were taken every other day, weather permitting, and from these, estimates of their drift were plotted. Slow and erratic, it was a complete disappointment at first. Nansen calculated that at this rate it would take them six to eight years to reach the Greenland Sea. There were times now when he began to doubt his own convictions. Maybe old Admiral Nares was right. Perhaps there was no such thing as an Arctic current after all. It might be nothing more than a general shifting of the winds and tides.

The thermometer comes to the surface. Deepwater temperatures were taken through holes cut in the ice.

Taking a sounding at 2058 fathoms

Week after week, the zigzag movements of the ship were plotted on a chart. Each time sightings were taken, the men gathered outside Scott-Hansen's cabin to await the results. Speculation ran from wild enthusiasm to downright despair. For the first few months, the answer was always the same; if they had not drifted back toward the south, they had indeed made very little progress forward. It was frustrating and disheartening, and it went on for the better part of a year.

With the coming of spring, the sun began to peer above the horizon and each day started its gradual climb up the blue-grey wall of sky. The climate changed, too, imperceptibly at first, then warmer and warmer until the ice and snow turned to slush, and wide areas of open water appeared like miniature blue lakes amid the white surroundings.

Bears were still very much in evidence, and occasionally the men came across a lone walrus wallowing in the open leads. As the days grew warmer, other visitors arrived, too: kittiwake gulls, fulmars, guillemots, skuas, snow buntings and the rare and beautiful little rose gull.

THE LONG DRIFT

All found the *Fram* an irresistible lure and a haven of safety during the occasional Arctic storms.

Nansen spent many hours dredging the open leads, collecting marine life, algae and diatoms, studying them under the microscope, classifying and describing them by the hundreds, adding considerably to the knowledge and understanding of Arctic biology.

From the standpoint of geography and oceanography, the most important result of the expedition was the discovery that the Arctic was a floating sea of ice. The many systematic soundings proved that it was a much deeper body of water than had first been anticipated, ruling out any possibility of a central land mass. It was the first conclusive answer to a riddle that had puzzled scientists for hundreds of years.

By the end of the first summer, their luck began to change. The drift toward the north began in earnest, and each day Hansen could actually plot another fraction of an inch on the chart. It was most encouraging, but judging from their present course Nansen realized now that instead of passing close in toward the North Pole, as he had hoped, they would actually drift slightly southeast, missing it by some hundreds of miles. With this in prospect, he began speculating on the possibility of a daring trek across the ice to reach it. He said nothing of this to the men; but as the months went by the idea intrigued him more and more, and he began making his plans.

The steady routine of work, the surprisingly comfortable ease of life made the little expedition one of the most successful voyages in the annals of Arctic exploration. It had been so well planned, so carefully organized, that there were few, if any, accidents or hardships. But in the early part of the second year, an incident occurred that almost brought the entire expedition to a tragic end.

It all started when a huge ice ridge began building up about 200 yards east of the *Fram*. Such ridges had formed many times before, and except for its large size this one caused little concern. Then, suddenly, activated by an unseen force, it began moving, bearing down directly on the ship. With the rumbling sound of distant thunder, great masses of ice shifted and heaved, piling up in erratic mountains of ice, toppling and tumbling over each other. The noise became louder, with sharp cracking and groaning strains as the ice fractured and split.

Sverdrup had just come below to warn Nansen of the impending danger when the ship was rocked by a heavy impact and began listing badly to port. Hurriedly, Nansen raced up the ladder, taking the steps by twos. When he reached the main deck, he was surprised to see the towering ledge of ice and snow looming over the *Fram*, ready to engulf it. Without a moment's hesitation, he ordered provisions and equipment taken ashore and stored in a place of safety where they would be available in the event the ship went down. Sleds, boats, clothing, food and barrels of fuel oil were quickly hauled out onto the ice, away from immediate danger.

The hours passed slowly as the ridge closed in like an iron vise, grinding and grumbling with a deafening racket. The dogs were led to safety, and the entire crew packed bags and personal belongings, as all hands made ready to abandon ship. For days the danger mounted, the ice pressing its persistent attack, crowding and shoving the ship until its timbers groaned and shook under the severe strain. Time and again, huge avalanches of snow and splintered ice fell across the

The "Fram" (Forward) forcing its way through the polar ice in the summer of 1895.

bows, scattering tons of debris across the deck. The *Fram* continued to list, but true to her design she resisted the relentless pressures.

Within another week, the ice released its hold, the crisis was over and it was evident that the *Fram* could hold her own against anything the Arctic had to offer.

Now, just as Nansen had predicted, the ship was drifting in a wide circle across the face of the Arctic, but from present calculations it was certain she would not cross the Pole. He began to think more and more about an attempt by dog sled. One afternoon, while they were out on a short skiing expedition, he told Sverdrup of his plans.

"The drift is going better than I had expected," he said. "Judging from our latest sightings, we should be a bit higher than 83 degrees, 34 minutes north."

"At this rate," said Sverdrup, "we ought to be close to the Pole by spring."

"Yes, but we'll still pass it by at least two or three hundred miles. It will take a sled journey to reach it."

Sverdrup glanced up, the thrill of anticipation shining in his eyes. "Then you still mean to make a try for it?"

"If everything goes well, I plan to leave the *Fram* sometime in early March."

"You'll not be going alone, of course?"

Nansen detected the ring of appeal in the old sailor's voice. He knew Sverdrup would give anything to be on the team that reached the Pole, but because he was needed here to command the *Fram* he would not be the one. "I've been thinking of taking Johansen," he said. "He's a superb athlete, he has great powers of endurance and he's an excellent skier. The others will stay here to carry on the work and to bring the *Fram* home safely." As he spoke, he saw the look of bitter disappointment in Sverdrup's face. "I know how you feel, Otto, but it's

THE LONG DRIFT

the only way. One of us has got to stay with the ship." He didn't tell Sverdrup that he was also thinking of his age. The man was almost forty-five, and Nansen felt that was a bit too old to go trudging off into the unknown.

Sverdrup nodded in understanding, a wan smile on his bearded face. "You're right, of course, we can't both go. But we've got to make sure that you have the best possible equipment. Once you leave the *Fram* your chances of finding it again will be quite slim."

Nansen agreed. "No, we'll not plan on coming back to the *Fram*. We'll head directly for the Pole, then on to Franz Josef Land. It's the nearest point of land and our only hope for survival."

Nansen pondered the matter for a few more days, then broached the subject to Johansen. The young man was delighted. "Of course, I'll go," he said. "Who wouldn't? It's the chance of a lifetime."

"Now, just a minute. I want you to think it over. You've got to be fully aware of what you're letting yourself in for."

"But I don't have to think it over," said Johansen, smiling. "I'm certain I want to go along."

"It will mean a great deal of hardship, and there will certainly be serious risks and dangers."

"I realize that."

"On the other hand," Nansen continued, "if you stay here you will be assured of a warm, comfortable berth while the *Fram* continues drifting out to the Atlantic. Then home to Norway and the welcome of the loved ones you left behind." Nansen stopped for a moment, then concluded. "If you go along with me, the outcome may be very different."

Johansen shook his head. "No, even if I thought it

over for another month, my answer would still be the same. I think it's a tremendous opportunity. I wouldn't miss it for the world."

Slowly, Nansen got to his feet, his heart filled with admiration for this young man who could so blithely place his life in the hands of another and for so hazardous a venture. "All right, then," he said. "It will be you and me. We may have to overcome some pretty formidable obstacles, but with luck and perseverance I'm sure we'll make it."

Word of the forthcoming expedition spread rapidly throughout the ship, and many of the men volunteered to go along. Lars Pettersen was one of them. "I know I'm not the best skier in the crew," he said. "But if you would be willing to take me along, I'm certain I could manage to keep up."

"I'm sorry, Lars," Nansen replied. "The work you are doing here is most important to the success of the expedition, and that's what counts at the present time. Besides, this trip to the Pole is not going to be any picnic."

"I know that, Sir. But none of us is going to live forever, so I'd be willing to take my chances. Besides, with you along to guide us, I'm sure we'd be able to see it through."

Nansen shook his head. "Thank you for your confidence, Lars, but I'm afraid the answer is still no. Getting the *Fram* back to Norway safely is far more important than reaching the Pole. I'm depending on you and the rest of the men to do just that. In the meantime, you can help by carrying on with your work and by helping us prepare the best possible equipment to do the job. Everything will depend on that."

"Well, Sir, of course I'll do everything I can to help

THE LONG DRIFT 141

make your trip comfortable and safe. And I'd like to add that you should be mighty careful and not take any unnecessary chances."

After Lars had left, Nansen went up on deck. For a long while he stood by the starboard bow, staring out over this vast wasteland of the Arctic, wondering why it held such a strange fascination for man and why, if necessary, so many of these young men were willing to give their lives for it. He knew the answer lay deep within himself, but the solution was still beyond his comprehension.

11

The Trek Toward the Pole

SLOWLY, A NEW ARCTIC DAY DAWNED, the sun climbed higher in the heavens and preparations for the daring race across the ice continued. Everyone pitched in. Mogstad constructed strong, flexible sleds. Sverdrup built kayaks and sewed up sleeping bags. Every expedient was used to save space and lighten the load the explorers would have to carry. The forms on which the kayaks were to ride were made out of pemmican stuffed into knitted bags and frozen into shape. These would serve as a reserve supply of food in the event of a shortage.

Dr. Blessing fitted up a small medicine kit and taught Nansen and Johansen the elements of first aid. Young Scott-Hansen sketched maps and charts to guide the travellers on their way, while Bentzen constructed leather harnesses for the dogs. It was to be a one-way,

THE TREK TOWARD THE POLE

all-out attempt to reach the Pole, a conquest that man had dreamed of for centuries. Now, as the day drew near, Nansen studied the maps and charts in an attempt to visualize the long, difficult terrain that lay ahead.

On March 14, 1895, the two men said good-bye to their companions and with three sleds, two kayaks and twenty-seven dogs started out across the ice. After an hour's march, Nansen finally looked back to see the distant silhouette of the *Fram*. With a tight feeling of nostalgia, he thought of the long hours he had spent in the warm, brightly lit cabins while the wind and snow howled outside. Now he was leaving that comfortable abode to press on into the mysterious unknown. With a visible effort, he waved a mittened hand, then turned around and set his face toward the north. The Pole was 360 miles away over some of the most difficult terrain on earth.

The weather was crystal clear with temperatures hovering around 35 degrees below zero. The first day they made 7 miles, then gradually increased the distance until they were covering 20 miles a day. Optimistic and confident, they trudged on, making camp each night, preparing a meal of hot chocolate, bread and pemmican.

But the first easy days of travelling did not last long. Soon, the ice turned into a nightmare of obstacles, a confused labyrinth of jagged blocks and crevasses. Undaunted, they struggled on across the troughs and over the ridges, making long detours around the frequent lanes of open water. At times they had to carry the floundering dogs over frozen hummocks 20 feet high, pulling the heavily loaded sleds up after them. It was a slow, gruelling pace, and at the end of each day they were bone-weary, barely able to keep themselves awake long enough to eat. They were advancing no more than a few miles a day now, and even the dogs were beginning to feel the strain. Some of them became weak and emanciated and, too feeble to go on, had to be killed, their thin carcasses serving as food for the others.

As day followed day, the explorers became satiated with the dull monotony of the dazzling white landscape, nothing but ice and snow stretching away to the distant horizon for thousands of miles. They stumbled on as if walking in a dream, their clothes saturated with the frozen accumulation of moisture from constant perspiration. What had started out as a bright, optimistic journey had bogged down into a dreary, agonizing death march.

The condition of the ice became, if anything, worse. Great ridges blocked their path now, compelling them to go out of their way, losing hours or days of precious time. Still, they forced themselves on, one painful step after another. Covering barely two or three miles a day, they were still hundreds of miles from their goal. The dogs were down to skin and bones now, footsore and so exhausted it was difficult to make them go on. The men coaxed and threatened, but the weakened animals could barely pull against the traces. All life and spirit seemed to be drained out of them. Some ran away; others simply lay down in the trail and refused to budge, preferring to be left behind than go on.

The two men were not in much better condition. Numb with cold and worn with fatigue, they frequently lay bundled up in their sleeping bags for hours at a time, trying to generate some warmth in their frozen bodies.

Each day, Nansen took sightings and made his calculations in order to determine their position. The results were disappointing and baffling, for in spite of their

THE TREK TOWARD THE POLE

efforts they seemed to be moving farther away from the Pole. Unwilling to give up, they continued, but after a few more days Nansen began to realize the reason for their failure. The entire ice mass on which they were travelling was drifting southward faster than they were moving north. The very current that had helped them penetrate this Arctic region was now sweeping them southward, away from their goal. For every step forward, they were drifting back two.

The situation was hopeless, and under the circumstances it would be sheer stupidity to go on fighting against something that was completely beyond their control.

So, after twenty-five days of bone-chilling misery, with more than half the dogs gone, Nansen decided to turn back. It was a difficult decision, but the only sensible one he could make. A meridian sighting indicated that they had reached 86 degrees, 13.6 minutes north, still 226 miles from the Pole but closer than any man had ever been before. On April 18, he climbed a tall ridge of ice and planted the Norwegian flag in the snow. Then, with heavy hearts, Nansen and Johansen turned south and headed for Franz Josef Land, 300 miles away.

Travelling in a direction parallel with the long ridges, they averaged 18 to 20 miles a day. But now the remainder of the dogs were failing under the gruelling pace, and one by one they fell behind and had to be killed. This was the most trying ordeal of the whole journey, for both Nansen and Johansen were fond of the faithful animals, and it was a heartrending experience to have to put them out of their misery.

With only two dogs left, the men carried on, putting their shoulders to the traces, hauling the heavily loaded sleds along by brute strength. Week after week, they

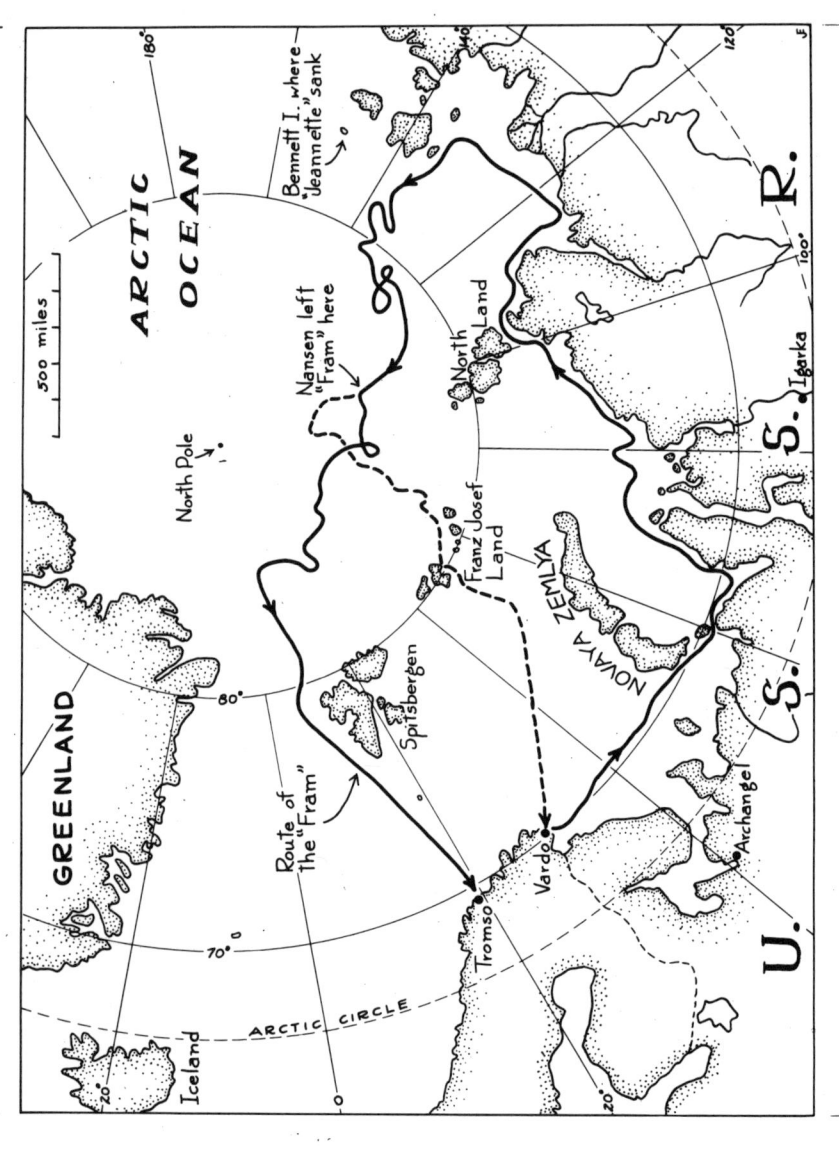

continued on under a blazing sun that turned the surrounding landscape into glaring white brilliance. Half-starved and utterly exhausted, they stumbled along, wondering if they would ever see home or loved ones again. When they were almost on the verge of falling in their tracks, they spotted the sweeping shadow of a lone fulmar circling in the sky. This was a good sign, for it meant that land or open water was not far away.

Sure enough, a few days later they came to a vast expanse of open sea. Here they pitched camp for a much-needed rest to prepare for the long journey across the water.

It was here that Johansen almost lost his life. He was repacking some gear when a huge polar bear jumped from behind a hummock and knocked him to the ground. Nansen heard the muffled cry and turned to see the huge beast standing over the stunned explorer, who was desperately trying to fend the animal off with his bare hands. Quickly, Nansen reached for his rifle, but it was wedged tightly under the bow of one of the kayaks. He pulled and yanked, but it would not come loose. In the meantime he heard Johansen shout, "You had better look sharp, or it will be too late."

Just at that moment, the bear spotted one of the sled dogs. It released Johansen to attack the smaller animal, giving Nansen time to extricate the gun. With careful aim, he fired, killing the animal instantly with a bullet through the brain. It was a close call and one that could easily have brought the little expedition to an untimely end.

The next morning found them paddling briskly through the open sea, the two kayaks lashed together, the sleds tied across the bows. At night, they would camp on the ice floes and each morning start out again. On

Travelling by kayak

July 24, 1895, they sighted their first range of mountains far off on the distant horizon, and a few days later they pulled the boats up on the rocky shore of Franz Josef Land.

It was over two years since they had left Norway and almost four months since they had last seen the *Fram*. For the moment, they were safe, but they knew they were still far from civilization and would have to face another grim winter in this cold, desolate land. Fortunately, here food was abundant. There were polar bears, seals, foxes, walruses and seabirds of every description, and they soon had an ample supply of fresh meat.

After a few days of rest, they set to work constructing a shelter in the side of a weathered cliff. Cutting deep into the soft stone, they built up the sides with moss and boulders, roofing it over with driftwood and walrus

THE TREK TOWARD THE POLE 149

hide. When it was finished, they stocked it with food, and like two hibernating animals they crawled in to spend the winter. In the gloomy silence of the little den, the days passed slowly, while the blizzards raged outside and prowling polar bears scratched at their door.

To relieve the monotony they memorized long lists of navigation tables and read and reread an old Norwegian almanac. To help while away the long hours they improvised word games. Unable to wash, they dreamed of hot Turkish baths. Without a change of clothes, they spent long hours talking of all the fancy shirts and jackets they would buy on their return to civilization. Subsisting on walrus fat and smoked polar bear meat, they conjured up visions of great platters of roast beef, gravy, brown potatoes, buttered peas, mushrooms, cakes, pies and pastries.

Occasionally, they managed to creep out of their hole to walk briskly up and down the beach and watch the thousands of shooting stars and the vivid displays of the aurora borealis lighting up the northern sky.

After what seemed like an eternity, the Arctic sun came out again, and the two explorers spent busy weeks getting gear and equipment ready for the last leg of their journey. They made sleeping bags, boots and clothing from polar bear skin. They shot walruses and seals and cut the meat into strips to tide them over for the first few weeks of the trip.

They had long since sacrificed the last of their two dogs, and on May 19, with boats lashed securely to the sleds, they started to work their way along the coast. For almost a month, they travelled by foot and by kayak, living off the land, shooting fulmars and seals. Once, Nansen almost lost his life when an angry bull walrus attacked his boat.

When travelling by kayak they usually lashed the two boats together, tying the sleds and equipment across the bows. If the wind was right, they hoisted a makeshift sail and went gliding smoothly across the water.

One evening, after they had been sailing all day, they pulled up to the edge of the ice in search of a high point from which they could get a better view of the surrounding country. Since the wind had died down, they did not bother to moor the boats but simply attached the lines to a halyard and threw them across the ice.

A short while later, they reached the top of a tall hummock and began looking around. Suddenly, Johansen cried out in alarm, "Look, the kayaks are adrift."

Sure enough, the wind had come up again, sweeping the light craft out into the water. Nansen raced down the hill, stripping off his outer garments as he ran. The kayaks were already some distance from shore, drifting rapidly before the wind. Without hesitation, he handed his watch to Johansen and plunged into the icy water.

He swam rapidly at first, with quick overhand strokes,

Heading southward, May 1896

making good time. But halfway out, the frigid water began to have its effect. His arms and legs became numb, and he began to feel weak and drowsy. With a supreme effort, he drove himself on, fighting against the dull numbness that was slowing him down.

As the minutes ticked by, he lost all sense of time and direction. He was so cold, so dazed he could hardly lift his arms, and he found it increasingly difficult to breathe. He knew now he would never make it. He would have to turn back.

But then the terrible reality of failure flashed through his mind. The drifting kayaks were carrying away all their worldly goods, their food, their guns and equipment. Without these, they could never reach civilization, they could never survive. The startling thought gave him renewed determination, and he continued on like a sleeping man floating in a cold, impossible dream. His muscles were knotted with cramps, and his frozen limbs refused to obey. It was almost as if he no longer possessed a body, as if his mind were merely drifting in the cold void of space.

Then, as if by some strange miracle, the dark outlines of the boats were a bit closer. By a sheer effort of will, he kicked and floundered, inching toward his goal. He was almost unconscious now, and he realized that if he didn't make it within the next few minutes it would be too late.

Through bleary, mist-filled eyes he looked up and saw the kayaks bobbing only a few feet away. He reached out feebly and missed, then tried again. This time, he caught hold of one of the snowshoes strapped across the bow. He hung on desperately, and little by little worked his way along the side of the boat. With a slow, agonizing effort, he managed to hook one leg over the edge and gradually pulled himself into the boat. Half-frozen

Half-frozen and utterly exhausted, Nansen reached the kayak and hooked one leg over the edge (drawing by A. Bloch)

and utterly exhausted, he lay there for a long while, panting deeply, trying to catch his breath.

When he had regained his strength, he picked up a paddle and started making his way back to shore, coming in some distance from Johansen. Just as the kayaks touched the edge of the floe, he noticed two auks sitting on the ice. Still dazed and only half-realizing what he was doing, he reached for his gun, killing both of them with one blast.

A few minutes later, Johansen came running up, thinking Nansen had gone mad. He helped him out of the boat, then quickly pulled off his wet clothing and packed him into one of the sleeping bags. His teeth chattering and his limbs trembling with the cold, Nansen waited for the warmth to creep back into his numb body.

THE TREK TOWARD THE POLE

A short distance away, he could hear the crackling of a warm fire and smell the tempting aroma of roasting waterfowl. His cold, blue lips broke into a wistful smile. They were safe, and he was certain now that they would find their way back to civilization. Once again, they had done the impossible.

They started out again, occasionally held up by inclement weather. But as soon as the storms had passed, they pushed on, hoping to reach Spitsbergen before the end of summer.

On June 17, as they were plodding along in the vicinity of Cape Flora, Nansen heard the sound of a barking dog. At first he thought it was merely his imagination, but minutes later he heard it again, clear and distinct. Leaving Johansen behind, he went on ahead and soon came upon a well-dressed man walking toward him across the ice. He was wearing an English tweed suit with high waterproof boots, and as he came closer Nansen recognized him immediately as the well-known British explorer, Frederick Jackson.

Upon meeting, the two men shook hands. For a long minute, Jackson stared at the ragged, begrimed figure of Nansen. Then, slowly, he realized who it was beneath the dirt and the long, scraggly beard. "I say," he exclaimed. "Aren't you Fridtjof Nansen?"

"Yes."

"By Jove," he said, pumping Nansen's hand. "I am glad to see you."

Nansen told him briefly about the *Fram* and about his unsuccessful attempt to reach the Pole.

"Congratulations," said the Englishman. "You've made a right good trip of it, though I'm afraid many of your colleagues have about given you up for lost."

A short while later, Johansen came up, and the two

men were taken back to Jackson's camp, where they had a hot bath and their first hot meal in almost a year.

It was pleasant to be back among companions again, to sit around a warm fire and chat about past adventures. But Nansen was anxious to get back to Norway in order to organize a search party in the event the *Fram* failed to turn up, and a month later he and Johansen were on their way home aboard Jackson's schooner, the *Windward*.

They reached Norway on August 13, landing at the little village of Vardo, where Nansen went directly to the local telegraph office. There he shoved a big stack of messages across the wooden counter. "I'd like to have these sent off at once," he said.

The clerk looked up at him with a quizzical frown, then down at the pile of telegrams. With a sudden start, he recognized the signature. Speechless, his mouth sagged open as the tremendous import of the occasion struck home. "You're Nansen," he gasped. "You're Fridtjof Nansen?"

Nansen nodded in reply.

The clerk turned to the telegraph operator. "Did you hear that," he shouted, "it's Fridtjof Nansen. He's alive, he's safe."

Quickly, the word spread, and soon the little telegraph office was filled with merchants and villagers who came to get a look at the long-lost explorers. The telegraph keys began to click, and the great news went out across the wires to inform a waiting world that Fridtjof Nansen was home.

As he was about to leave, the clerk informed him that his good friend Professor Henrick Mohn was staying at the local hotel. Without waiting to hear more, Nansen ran up the street and burst open the door to Mohn's apartment. The old man was lying on the sofa, smoking

Nansen was 36 when this photograph was taken in London, and already famous for his exploration of the Polar Sea.

his pipe and reading. He jumped up quickly as Nansen entered, a startled expression on his round face. His pipe fell from his mouth, and he stared as though he were seeing a ghost.

"Good heavens, it can't be," he mumbled.

Nansen never moved. He stood in the doorway, quietly smiling.

The tears started down Mohn's big cheeks as he wept unashamedly. "Fridtjof Nansen, my God, you're alive!" With that, he rushed into Nansen's open arms, hugging him like a brother.

That night, they had a joyous reunion — Nansen, Mohn and Johansen. Nansen told how they had left the *Fram* at the 84th parallel. "She was in perfect condition," he said, "drifting rapidly past the Pole. My one hope is that she will reach the Greenland Sea before another winter and will make her way home."

But Nansen did not have to wait until winter. A week later, he was staying at Hammerfast with his family and friends when a message arrived. With trembling fingers, Nansen opened the telegram and read the startling news.

FRAM ARRIVED IN GOOD CONDITION. ALL WELL ON BOARD. SHALL START AT ONCE FOR TROMSO. WELCOME HOME!

OTTO SVERDRUP

With the small group of friends gathered around him, Nansen made the momentous announcement, "The *Fram* has arrived." It was all he could say.

Yes, the *Fram* had arrived. Steaming into Skjaervo, Norway, on August 20, 1896, she had completed one of the most fantastic voyages ever attempted by man — a 2,000-mile drift across the top of the world from New

Siberia to the Atlantic Ocean. On August 13, after more than three years of drifting, she had reached the edge of the Greenland Sea, where Sverdrup blasted her out of the ice and set his course for home. Once again, Nansen's planning and foresight had accomplished the impossible.

The drift of the *Fram* was a unique achievement in the annals of exploration. The huge mass of scientific work accomplished on board contributed to the fields of meteorology, oceanography, geography, biology and physics. Years later, when the work of compiling the results was completed, it filled six large volumes. It was the most comprehensive and intensive research of the Arctic regions ever attempted, and its like was not surpassed until 62 years later when 54 nations participated in the International Geophysical Year of 1957.

But for now, the long years of isolation and solitude were over. Nansen was happy, and he was home once again with his beloved Eva and little Liv. Letters and congratulations began to pour in from all over the world, from presidents and kings, from learned societies and fraternal organizations. Nansen was hailed as one of the greatest explorers of the twentieth century. Everywhere he went, people crowded about him, greeting him with a hero's welcome. Bands played, flags were unfurled and his path was strewn with flowers. He was the man of the hour. To Norway, he was the man of the century.

The parades, celebrations and orations continued for weeks. He was invited to speak as a distinguished guest in England, in Europe, in America, in virtually every civilized country of the world. Many of the invitations he accepted; most of them he was forced to decline. It was humanly impossible to fulfill them all, even for such an energetic man as Nansen.

12

The Last Great Adventure

AFTER THE FIRST MONTHS OF FESTIVITIES, Nansen again tried to escape the unwelcome glare of publicity. His only wish was to get back to his work, to live in peace and quiet with his family. He succeeded for a while, serving as professor of zoology at Christiania and sailing out on short oceanographic expeditions into the Atlantic.

Then, in 1905, an incident occurred that changed the entire course of his life. The bold, daring adventurer had now become a wise humanitarian, an elder statesman of peace.

For hundreds of years, the tiny Norwegian nation had been ruled by the strong, dominant hand of Sweden. Now, with a new surge of confidence, the Norwegian people wanted their independence. The situation was tense; troops and cannon were mobilized along the border. War seemed imminent, and Nansen was called upon to lead the cause for freedom. His magnetic per-

THE LAST GREAT ADVENTURE

sonality, the magic of his name would lead the patriots to victory. But Nansen did not resort to arms. Instead, he travelled to the capitals of Europe, writing, pleading, seeking support. The statesmen of Europe flocked to hear him speak. The clarity of his arguments, the logic of his cause convinced them of his nation's merit. Sweden herself agreed, and the crisis was settled peacefully, without bloodshed or violence. Norway became an independent state.

Back in 1889, when Nansen had first ridden through the streets of Christiania the conquering hero of Greenland, a small boy stood on the sidelines cheering along with the crowd. His name was Roald Amundsen, and he, too, had a burning desire to be an explorer. Now, sixteen years later, he came to Nansen to ask for the loan of the *Fram*. He wanted to organize an oceanographic expedition to the Arctic and at the same time make another attempt on the Pole.

Nansen hesitated. He had plans of his own, many of which included the *Fram*. Not wishing to discourage the young man, he told Amundsen he would think it over. A year later, he was working in his study when word came that Amundsen was downstairs in the drawing room waiting for his answer. Nansen got up, sighing heavily, still undecided. He knew his decision might make the difference between success or failure in the young man's career, and he thought back to the days when he, too, needed help. Yet, he still had his own plans to think about.

As he started for the stairs, he met Eva on the landing. She reached out and put her hand on his arm. "I know what this means," she said. "You will be leaving me again."

For a long moment, Nansen stared off into the distance,

deep in thought. Then he patted her hand gently and continued down the stairs. He went immediately to Amundsen, greeting him cordially. In a quiet voice, he said, "Yes, you may have the *Fram*."

A few years later, Nansen stood on the balcony of his home as he watched the *Fram* sail out to sea. Her pennants were waving in the breeze, and on the bridge stood Roald Amundsen, headed for the Pole. Nansen had stayed home to be with his wife, but in the meantime she had died. Now, in 1910, he was alone, and the *Fram* was sailing without him. It was the bitterest moment of his life.

Not long after, in 1914, came the distant echoes of World War I, and Norway found herself in a precarious position. Surrounded by U-boats and strangled by a blockade, she was struggling for her very existence. Once again, Nansen was asked to use his influence as a diplomat. He travelled to London, Washington and other world capitals, working out ways and agreements that would bring Norway the food and supplies she must have to survive.

With the coming of peace in 1919, he turned back to his work, but not for long. This time a call came from the newly formed League of Nations, asking him to help with the repatriation of war prisoners. Almost reluctantly, he accepted and was soon involved in this new humanitarian effort, completely forgetting his own interests and ambitions.

Hundreds of thousands of prisoners were still being held in Russian prison camps, and the Soviet government showed little concern for their health or safety. Thousands were starving and other thousands were dying of disease.

Nansen went directly to Moscow to see Grigori V.

Chicherin, the Russian foreign minister. After a long wait, he was admitted into a cold, austere office, where he explained the purpose of his mission.

Chicherin frowned. "No, Dr. Nansen, we do not recognize your League of Nations, so I am afraid it is impossible for us to negotiate."

"But these men are dying of hunger," said Nansen. "Thousands of them. If we do not do something, soon it may be too late."

The foreign minister shrugged. "The Russian people are starving, too. We have just come through a bloody revolution. Our entire economy is disrupted. What little is left belongs to the people. We do not propose to give it away to our enemies."

Nansen winced. He could see that Chicherin was not to be moved by compassion. He would have to think of something else if he were to succeed. He was quiet for a moment, pacing back and forth, pondering this cruel dilemma. Suddenly, he turned. "Suppose I act on my own," he said. "Not as a representative of the League or any other organization, but strictly on my own, without conditions or formalities."

Chicherin nodded slowly. "It's a bit irregular," he said. "But perhaps we might be able to arrange something on that basis."

Nansen felt a new surge of hope.

"However," said Chicherin, "there is still the matter of money. Who is to pay for all this?"

"I'll get in touch with the Red Cross and other charitable groups. I'm sure I can get the necessary backing."

"Good," said Chicherin. "I think we can do business. I will see what I can do about transport. But only as far as the border, mind you. You will have to take over from there."

Nansen went out and moved mountains. He begged

and he pleaded, he pulled strings and used his influence, and finally he got the money he needed. The Russians kept their word. Two trains each day reached the western frontier, jam-packed with prisoners. In all, Nansen repatriated 427,000 men, at the fantastically low rate of $8.60 per man.

This emergency had barely been settled when another call came from the League of Nations, this time to help rescue the million and a half refugees still wandering across Europe, fleeing from one country to another. Once again, Nansen got to work, coaxing, persuading, arranging for jobs, homes and medical treatment and getting the refugees resettled in their new land. It was a herculean task, spread over a vast area, but he kept at it with determination and patience.

When the problem of passports came up, threatening to impede the whole operation, he promptly designed a passport of his own. It became known as a Nansen Certificate and was eventually recognized by more than fifty countries all over the world.

In the midst of all this, another flood of refugees was loosed upon Europe as the result of the Greco-Turkish War. Nansen was an old hand at this by now, and he soon had repatriation headquarters set up in various areas of the troubled zones. Thousands of Turks were relocated in Asia, and more than a million Greeks were reestablished in their own homeland. All of this was done with minimal funds and only the flimsiest kind of support. Frequently, Nansen even rolled up his sleeves and pitched in with the cooking, the distribution of food and clothing and other necessary tasks. As the years went by, his name became a household word throughout Europe, and millions of children went to bed each night remembering him in their prayers.

The famous Nansen Passport which the explorer invented so that stateless people might travel to countries where there was some prospect of work. This passport was honored by more than fifty governments and carried by such distinguished people as the pianist Rachmaninoff and the dancer Anna Pavlova.

Nansen tastes the food in a Near East Relief orphanage during a visit to Armenia on behalf of Armenian refugees.

Each time Nansen tried to turn back to his work, a new call came from a troubled land, a call that he could not refuse. Now a terrible famine swept across Russia, leaving 30,000,000 peasants without food or sustenance. Death and starvation were stalking the land, and people were eating leaves, bark, straw, even dogs and cats. Nansen went to the league for funds, but this time his request was flatly rejected. Russia's predicament was of her own making, they said. Now she must bear the consequences of her acts.

This was partly true, but Nansen was a humanitarian, not a politician. The degradation and suffering he saw in Russia shocked his sensibilities and filled him with a grim determination. He stumped through Europe and America, lecturing, pleading, showing slides — grim, horrible pictures of the anguish and misery, the stark reality of pestilence and famine in a dark and backward land.

THE LAST GREAT ADVENTURE 165

Then the money began rolling in — from France, from Holland and Scandinavia, from private organizations and societies, from the Vatican, from all over Europe. In America, the children broke open their penny banks and turned the money over to schools and collection agencies. The Hoover Relief Commission worked with Nansen, sending food, clothing and medical supplies amounting to sixty million dollars. Nansen gave full credit to his American colleague. "In the entire history of the world," he said, "there is no humanitarian effort that can compare with the relief work organized by Herbert Hoover."

As the years passed, Nansen became a familiar figure at the League of Nations, fighting for the rights and freedom of the smaller nations all over the world. In

Nansen in his later years. The great humanitarian died at Oslo on May 13, 1930.

1922 he received the Nobel Prize for peace and promptly turned the money over to the Greek and Russian relief agencies.

In addition to his many achievements, Nansen also holds an important place in the history of his country's literature. His travels in the Arctic resulted in such books as *In Northern Mists*, a comprehensive history of Arctic exploration from earliest times, and *Farthest North*, published in 1898, a thrilling account of the drift of the *Fram* and a classic of polar exploration. The story of his youthful days with Krefting aboard the *Viking* is told in *Hunting and Adventure in the North* and contains important contributions to the fields of zoology and natural history. His books, *Armenia and the Near East*, *Through Siberia* and *Through the Caucasus to the Volga* are based on his observations while working with the refugees in Russia and the Near East.

He was the author of scores of scientific research papers, ranging from oceanography and marine biology to geology and ethnology. True to the teachings of his old friend, Professor Mohn, he was never idle, never at a loss for something to do. His agile mind found interest in everything and anything that crossed his path. His curiosity was as big as all outdoors; his work was all around him.

During all these years, he had never given up his interest in science and exploration and kept dreaming of the day when he could return to the Arctic. Now he was free once more and, at the age of sixty-nine, he got out his maps and charts and dusted them off. This time he had drawn up detailed plans to fly over the North Pole in a dirigible, a risky venture in 1917. As always, it was a unique and daring scheme that enticed him.

But his long years of effort on behalf of suffering

The "Fram" in the Museum at Oslo

humanity had left him worn and exhausted. On a warm, sunny afternoon in May of 1930, he was sitting in front of his home, gazing out across the fjord toward the distant mountains that he loved so well, when suddenly his head fell forward on his chest. He sighed deeply, his eyes closed and a moment later he was dead.

The entire world mourned his passing. He had made adventure a noble undertaking; he had been the inspiration and guiding light for others to follow. As a scientist, he was the first to map the Arctic ice cap and probe its unknown depths. He laid the foundation for polar meteorology and proved the existence of a powerful Arctic current.

As a humanitarian, he brought order and stability out of chaos and misery. Almost single-handed, he saved hundreds of thousands of lives and brought new hope and dignity to millions of others. And he died as he had lived, still looking ahead, still planning for the next great adventure.

Today, at Bygdoy, Norway, not far from Oslo, the *Fram* stands on display. Restored to her original condition and installed in an old-style Viking boat shed, she is visited each year by thousands of sightseers, from schoolchildren and tourists to ambassadors and heads of state. Her sturdy frame and rugged lines are fitting tribute to the man who once commanded her helm, Fridtjof Nansen.

Bibliography

Brogger, W. C., and Rolfsen, N. *Fridtjof Nansen, 1861–1893.* London: Longmans, Green, 1896.
Hoyer, Liv Nansen. *A Family Portrait.* London: Longmans, Green, 1957.
Johansen, Hjalmar. *With Nansen in the North.* London: Longmans, Green, 1899.
Nansen, Fridtjof. *First Crossing of Greenland.* London: Longmans, Green, 1890.
———. *Farthest North.* New York: Harper Bros., 1897.
———. *Hunting and Adventure in the Arctic.* New York: Duffield, 1925.
Nansen, Fridtjof (ed.). *The Norwegian North Polar Expedition.* 6 vols. London: Longmans, Green, 1900–06.
Reynolds, E. F. *Nansen.*

London: Harmondsworth, Penguin Books, 1949.
Shackleton, Edward. *Nansen the Explorer.*
London: H. F. & G. Witherby, 1959.
Sorenson, Jon. *The Saga of Fridtjof Nansen.*
New York: W. W. Norton, 1932.

COLLECTED BIOGRAPHY

Ludwig, Emil. *Nine Etched from Life.*
New York: Robert M. McBride, 1934.
Mitchell, J. Leslie. *Earth Conquerors.*
New York: Simon & Schuster, 1934.

Index

Aars (headmaster), 24, 25
America, 116, 157, 164, 166
Amundsen, Anton, 123
Amundsen, Roald, 159, 160
Archer, Colin, 111-113, 125
Arctic Circle, 117
Arctic current, 101, 106-108, 133, 145, 168
Arendal, Norway, 19, 54
Armenia and the Near East, 166
Atlantic Ocean, 157, 158
aurora borealis, 131, 149
Australia, 116

Balto, Samuel Johannesen, 78, 80, 83, 86, 91, 95
Bentzen, Bernt, 123
Bergen, Norway, 56, 59, 68, 117
Bergen Museum, 54, 68
Bering Strait, 107
Blessing, Dr. Henrik, 124, 133, 142
Brogger, Prof. W.C., 61-67
Bygdoy, Norway, 168

Cape Dan, Greenland, 65, 75

Cape Farewell, 82
Challenger, HMS, 105
Chicherin, Grigori V., 160, 161
Christiania Fjord, 15
Christiania, Norway, 16, 17, 20, 27, 34, 55, 56, 68, 69, 72, 95
Christianshaab, Greenland, 65
Christmas, 55, 130, 131
Cleve, Prof. (of Upsala), 107
Collett, Prof. R., 28, 54, 55
Copenhagen, 19, 77, 94, 95

Danielssen, Dr. D., 55, 59
Dietrichson, Oluf, 76, 90, 91
Discovery, HMS, 105
Disko Bay, Greenland, 65, 88
dolphins, 30, 43
dovekites, 41
ducks, 21, 25, 117
England, 99, 114, 157
Eric the Red, 96
Eskimos, 72, 85, 102
Europe, 99, 111, 114, 116, 124, 157, 159, 162, 164, 165
Farthest North, 166
Fram, 113, 115-117, 121-128, 130-132, 135, 136, 138,
139, 143, 148, 153, 154, 156, 157, 159, 160, 166, 168
France, 165
Franklin, Sir John, 22
Franz Josef Land, 139, 145, 148
Fredricksdal, Greenland, 84
fulmars, 32, 41, 134, 147, 149

Gamel, Augustin, 73, 93, 94
gannets, 31
Godthaab, Greenland, 89, 92, 93
Godthaab (Nansen's home in Norway), 102, 115, 116
Golgi, Prof. C., 59
Great Fröen, 20, 27, 55
Greco-Turkish War, 162
Greeks, 162, 166
Greenland, 52, 58, 59, 62-64, 69, 70, 72, 76, 79, 80, 91, 92, 97, 159
Greenland Sea, 133
Grieg, Dr. Lorentz, 59
guillemots, 33, 41, 134
Gustav, Karl, of Sweden, 19

Hammerfast, Norway, 156
Hansen, Scott-, *see* Scott-

INDEX

Hansen
Henriksen, Peter, 117, 119, 121, 129
Holland, 165
Hooker, Sir Joseph D., 109
Hoover, Herbert, 166
Hoover Relief Commission, 166
Hunting and Adventure in the North, 166

Inglefield, Adm. Edward, 105
In Northern Mists, 166
International Geographical Congress, 99
International Geophysical Year, 157
Italy, 59, 97
Ivitut, Greenland, 93

Jackson, Frederick, 153, 154
Jacobsen, Capt., 77
Jacobsen, Theodore, 123
Jan Mayen Islands, 34, 43
Jason, 75, 78, 92
Jeannette Expedition, 106
Johansen, Hjalmar, 116, 130, 131, 138, 139, 142, 145, 147, 150, 152, 153, 156

Juell, Adolf, 117, 119-121, 124, 130

Kara Sea, 117
Khabarova, Russia, 117
Krefting, Capt. Alex, 16, 18, 31, 32, 40, 42, 47, 50, 52, 53, 166
Kristiansen, Kristian, 77

Lapland, 78, 79
League of Nations, 160, 161, 162, 166
London, 105, 160

Magnus, King, 96
Markham, Commo. Albert, 105
McClintock, Sir Leopold, 105, 107, 110
Mineralogical Institute, Stockholm, 61
Mogstad, Ivar, 123, 129, 142
Mohn, Prof. H., 29, 63, 69-71, 73, 74, 82, 101, 106, 154, 156, 166
Moscow, 160

Nansen, Alexander, 20, 21, 90
Nansen Certificate, 162
Nansen, Baldur, 19-20, 54-56, 59
Nansen, Eva Sars, 96-104, 115, 131
Nansen, Hans, 19
Nansen, Liv, 102, 115, 131, 157
Nansen, Fridtjof, description of, 15; meets Krefting, 16-18; boyhood, 20-27; enters college, 27; boards Viking, 28; seal hunting, 36-46; marksmanship, 38; leads hunt, 40; marine studies, 41; attack by seal, 46; trapped in ice, 47; hunts polar bears, 48-51; at Bergen Museum, 54-56; in Italy, 59; works on thesis, 59; meets Brogger and Nordenskjold, 62-67; skis across Norway, 68, 69; prepares for Greenland expedition, 73, 74; sails aboard the *Jason*, 75-78; sketches glaciers, 81; falls through crevasse, 86; trek across ice cap, 85-92; return to Norway, 94-96; meets Eva Sars, 96, 97; married, 99; receives Vega medal, 100; writes book on Greenland, 100; plans for Polar expedition, 104-110; builds *Fram*, 111-113; sails for Pole, 115; hunts walrus, 117-121; drives sled dogs, 126-128; observes aurora borealis, 131; studies marine life, 135; plans trek to Pole, 138-140; leaves *Fram*, 143; turns back, 145; spends winter in hut, 148-149; rescues kayaks, 150-152; reaches Cape Flora, 153; meets Jackson, 153; home to Norway, 154; hailed as hero, 157; becomes diplomat, 158; lends *Fram* to Amundsen, 159; works for refugees, 160-162; helps Russians, 164-166; wins Nobel Prize, 166; dies, 168
Nares, Adm. George, 105, 108, 133
Near East, 166
New Siberia Islands, 106, 156, 157
Nobel Prize, 166
Nordahl, Bernhard, 124

INDEX

Nordenskjold, Baron Adolph, 35, 58, 60, 63-67
Nordmarka, 20-21, 25, 90
Northeast Passage, 35, 64
North Pole, 101, 107, 135, 138-140, 145, 166
Norway, 96, 116, 117, 131, 154, 158-160

Ommanney, Adm. Erasmus, 105
Oscar, King (of Sweden), 100

Pettersen, Lars, 123, 140, 141
plankton, 41, 135
polar bears, 28, 47, 117, 126, 129, 130, 134, 147-149
ptarmigan, 21, 26, 40

Rae, Dr. John, 105
Ravna, Ole N., 78-80, 83
Red Cross, 161
Royal Geographic Society, 104, 105, 110
Russia, 160, 161, 164, 166
Russians, 162

Scandinavia, 94, 111, 165
Scott-Hansen, 116, 123, 130, 131, 134, 135
seals, 34-37, 42, 46, 47, 144, 148, 149
Sermilik Fjord, 75
sharks, 47
Skagerrak, 30, 116
Skjaervo, Norway, 156
sled dogs, 117, 126-130, 136, 143-145, 149
snow bunting, 91, 134
Spitsbergen, 64, 153
Stockholm, Sweden, 60, 64
sukas, 83, 134
Svartebukta, Norway, 100
Sverdrup, Otto, 75, 78, 80-83, 86, 88, 89, 92, 93, 95, 98, 116, 122, 136, 138, 142, 156
Sweden, 96, 158, 159
Swedish Anthropological and Geographical Society, 100

Through the Caucasus to the Volga, 166
Through Siberia, 166
Tromsö, Norway, 117
Turks, 162

Umivik Fjord, 85

Vardo, Norway, 117, 154
Vatican, 165
Vega, 35
Vega medal, 100
Viking, 18, 19, 29, 30, 32, 34, 35, 40, 42-44, 47, 52, 53, 166
Voss, Norway, 68

walruses, 117-121, 134, 148, 149
Washington, D.C., 160

Wedel family, 19
whales, 28, 42, 43, 59
Wharton, Capt., 105
White Sea, 19
Wiggins, Capt. Joseph, 105
Windward, 154
World War I, 160
Wrangel Island, 106

Young, Sir Allen, 105, 108

Zoological Station (Naples, Italy), 59